D1625415

HARD
FIGHTING
SOLDIER

To Yolanda

"Prov 3:5-6"

War Eagle & God Bless

Bro. Chitt.
2007

HARD
FIGHTING
SOLDIER

Finding God in Trials, Tragedies, and Triumphs

CHETTE WILLIAMS

Chaplain, Auburn University Football Team

with
DICK PARKER

Looking Glass Books

Unless otherwise noted, Scripture taken from the Holy Bible,
New International Version, © 1973, 1978, 1984 International Bible Society.
Used by permission of Zondervan.

Also quoted:
The New American Standard Bible (NASB),
© 1960, 1962, 1963, 1968, 1971, 1972, 1973, 1975, 1977, 1995
by The Lockman Foundation.

New King James Version (NKJB), © 1982 by Thomas Nelson, Inc.

The Holy Bible, King James Version (KJV).

Published by
Looking Glass Books, Inc.
Decatur, Georgia

Jacket artwork by Steve Penley
Jacket design by Burtch Bennett Hunter

Manufactured in the United States of America

ISBN 978-1-929619-31-3

For Lakeba, my rock in this world,
and my parents,
Katie and Calvin Williams Sr.,
and Lakeba's mother,
Stella Hibbler

FOREWORD

By Tommy Tuberville

Head Football Coach, Auburn University

It's almost game time. The players have gone through their pregame stretches on the field and heard last-minute instructions from their position coaches. Now they're back in the locker room making final mental preparations. Over to one side I see Chette Williams, "Brother Chette," the players call him, kneeling in prayer with a player. When he says amen, another steps over. Prayer has become a vital part of these young men's lives, even in the final moments before each game.

When I came to Auburn as head football coach in 1999, I accepted responsibility for helping 120 young men grow into conscientious adults—the whole person, not just the athlete. It's an ongoing process from the time they come here until they leave, and even thirty years from now they can still call on us. I knew my assistant coaches and I would need help, and what better person to have than a man of the Lord who played football at Auburn and knows what these players go through? Chette Williams understands their aches and pains, their problems away from football, and all the situations and temptations that can arise. He's been there. Now Chette's ministry is a major part of how we build a football team and help young men grow to young adults.

Chette has a special way of reaching others. He doesn't spend a lot of time preaching sermons. Instead, he listens. He comes to practices, workouts, and team meetings, making himself available when players need a guide. They all know they can call Brother Chette or come see him any time. He's not a miracle worker. He's just a man who understands and who knows the Lord. Ask a player what Chette means to him, and he's likely to say, "He's like a father. He's always there for me." In that way Chette is modeling our Lord and leading these young men into a closer relationship with Him.

In *Hard Fighting Soldier*, Chette tells how God has changed his life and continues to touch the lives of players and coaches. Read it and let Him touch your life as well.

CONTENTS

A Prodigal 1

The Rotten Nature of Self Reliance 5

When We Were the Least of These 9

The Elusive Big Time 13

Recruiting for the Lord 20

Putting the Temple on Display 23

God's Game Plan 29

Into the Desert 36

Bridging the Chasm 42

Through Kyle's Eyes 46

One Day at a Time 50

Seeking Comfort in the Death of a Teammate 55

Restoring the Years 61

Changing Seasons 65

Time to Give It All 72

Scars of the Wounded 76

Singing a New Song in Unison 85

God's Plans 88

Loose the Bonds 95

A New Day Dawning 100

Calling on His Name 107

From the Mountaintop of Prayer To the Valley of Temptation 114

He Will Not Forget 119

Don't Come Home Empty-Handed 125

A Handful of Mustard Seeds 130

Surrender and Trust 135

Learning to Forgive 140

Hard Fighting Soldiers 144

A Bigger Stage 148

Praise Report at Twenty 151

An Audience of One 161

Sending Forth 174

HARD
FIGHTING
SOLDIER

Football is a violent game, and Chette was a violent man—a very aggressive football player. His effort and personality on the football field were exactly what you're looking for. But he had that same personality off the field, and sometimes that's not conducive to getting along.

Pat Dye
Auburn head football coach, 1981–92

I'm sitting there as a graduate assistant coach working with the scout team, and I look over and see that Chette is almost in a physical fight with [coach] Wayne Hall. And I think, *That is the most miserable-looking young man I have ever seen.* As the scene unfolds, my next thought is, *This guy's got to go. He's just got an attitude.*

John Gibbons
Auburn graduate assistant coach, 1982

Chette was intimidating when I was a freshman at Auburn. I thought he'd be the one in prison. I'm telling you, I was scared of Chette.

Demetrius Cotchery
Auburn linebacker, 1982
Inmate No. 214437, Staton Correctional Facility

Chette lockered next to me in the walk-on locker room. He was a mean, bitter, angry-looking guy. And a little scary. I tried to talk with him, and he wouldn't even respond. I told the other guys in FCA that I was going to pray for Chette, and they said, "You've got to be kidding! Come on, you don't need to pray for that guy. He's a lost cause. Pray for somebody you can have some success with."

Kyle Collins
Auburn running back, 1982–85

1

A PRODIGAL

"Not long after that, the younger son got together all he had, set off for a distant country, and there squandered his wealth in wild living. After he had spent everything, there was a severe famine in that whole country, and he began to be in need."

LUKE 15:13–14

They said I was a lost cause. Not even worth praying for.

Coach Dye must have agreed, because one night near the end of my sophomore season at Auburn University, I came back to the dorm late. I guess it was an hour or so after curfew, and I'd had a beer or two. I had just flopped onto the bed in my underwear when a knock came at the door. Nobody but another player living in the Sewell Hall, the athletic dorm, would knock at that time of night.

"Come in," I said.

The door pushed open, and it was Coach Daniel, the assistant offensive line coach. I hated James Daniel. I thought he was a hatchet man for Coach Pat Dye. He and two other coaches lived in the dorm and seemed to watch us all the time, just looking for us to get in trouble. I reached down to pick up my pants and stumbled a little standing up.

"Out late," he said.

"I lost track of the time," I said without looking up.

"Studying?"

"Yeah, studying."

He snickered sarcastically. I pulled up my pants and sat back down.

It wasn't the first time Coach Daniel had knocked on my door, and every time it meant trouble—usually stadiums. I'd lost count of the times I had run up and down all forty-six aisles of the lower stands in Jordan-Hare Stadium with a concrete block on my back. If it was raining, I ran coliseums instead—twenty-five at a time. Up and down all the way around the basketball arena was one. Always with the concrete block strapped to my back. It was wrapped in a towel to keep it from ripping my skin. They got me for skipping class, staying out late, fighting Coach Wayne Hall, and fighting another player. Nobody was in better shape than Pat Dye's troublemakers. They said Auburn lacked discipline before he came. Not anymore. We ran until we threw up. Then we got up and ran some more until we passed out.

"Coaches had a meeting today," Daniel said.

"Yeah?"

"You were on the agenda."

In an instant I was sober. Me? Why would the whole coaching staff be talking about me? It was either really good or really bad, and since I'd been kicked off the travel squad for the Florida game, I figured it must be really bad. Or was Daniel bluffing? I looked hard, but he didn't blink. Didn't give a clue.

Then he made it quick. "Chette," he said, "you're a problem. A bad seed. You've been here nearly two seasons, and we've never seen you smile. Nobody works harder than you in the weight room and on the practice field. Nobody is more committed on the field than you. But then you mess it all up with your attitude. You stay out late, you come home drunk or high, and you're on academic probation. You argue and fight with your coaches and your teammates. We thought dropping you from the travel squad last week would straighten you out, but here you are out late again."

I looked up at him. This was his "one-last-chance" speech, and I wanted to look him in the eye when he said it. He needed to know I was a man, and when I said I would straighten up, he needed to believe it. I believed it myself. I knew what he was saying was true, and I didn't like it. It was time to straighten myself up and show them the real Chette Williams.

My older brother Quency had gotten the one-last-chance speech right before they suspended him from the team for a quarter. I started thinking about what I would do for the next three months and how I would keep Mama from finding out I'd been suspended.

"Chette," Coach Daniel said, "we think it's time for you to move on."

I stared at him and waited for him to finish his sentence with, ". . . for a while." But he just stood there and didn't say anything else— nothing about how long or when I would be back.

Finally I asked, "What do you mean?"

"I mean you're off the team."

Off the team, I thought. *No, that can't be right. This can't be happening. Tell me this isn't happening. Off the team? Are you sure?* My stomach rolled like I was about to get sick, and I lowered my head. "I understand," I said, but I didn't.

I didn't hear much else he said, just pieces of sentences: "I'm sorry, Chette . . . other programs, other schools . . . we can help . . . not a good fit for you or for us." He must have known I wasn't listening, because after a while the room was quiet and he was gone.

I rolled over on the bed and stared at the wall. Other schools? Other programs? What was he talking about? Auburn was *my* school. It was the *only* program.

I pulled the pillow up under my head, and in that instant I knew I was the lost son, the prodigal. Except I had no father to go home to. Calvin Williams Sr. was even more lost than I was. I had hardly spoken to him in nearly two years, since he and Mama divorced. The closest man I had to a father right now was Coach Dye, and he had just kicked me off the team.

Maybe I *was* a lost cause.

2

THE ROTTEN NATURE
OF SELF-RELIANCE

He did not do many mighty works there because of their unbelief.
MATTHEW 13:58 (NKJV)

I lay on the bed staring at the ceiling. How does a good kid become a "bad seed," the kind of man who gets kicked off his football team?

At Douglas County High School, I had been one of Coach Jimmy Johnson's favorite players—the hardest-working guy on the team. He said he loved coaching the Williams brothers (five of my six brothers also played for him), because we were so disciplined. "If they ever get out of line," he said more than once, "I don't have to do anything but tell them I'll have to have a talk with Miss Katie." That was my mother, Katie Williams. Everybody who knew her respected her for raising seven well-behaved boys while our father was on the road driving a tractor-trailer rig all week. I was twelve years old the last time she whipped me. I think she might have caught me with a cigarette.

"You go get me a hickory switch, Chette Williams."

"Aw, Mama."

"Don't you 'Aw, Mama' me. You get out there and find me a switch."

I sighed and dragged myself out the back door and started looking. There was an art to finding the right switch. Too big and Mama would rip my legs to shreds. Too small and she'd send me back for something bigger, and she'd be madder than ever. She said *switch*, but what she meant was *limb*. I found a low-growing limb and twisted it until it broke off, then stripped the leaves one at a time. Mama was standing over the kitchen sink when I opened the back door slowly and tiptoed into the house. She heard me.

"Go to your bedroom and get those pants off."

"Aw, Mama!"

She turned off the water and stared at me. I drug the limb back to my room and pulled down my jeans. She was right behind me.

"Lean over."

I stretched out across the bed, and she grabbed the limb and whipped me. I didn't cry or make a sound; I gritted my teeth as the thunder slapped my skin and the lightning bolt shot all the way up my spine. She didn't quit until I had more stripes on my legs than she could count.

Sometimes her methods were less painful but equally effective. One morning one of my brothers called from the bedroom, "Mama, I can't go to school today. I'm sick."

"That's okay, baby," Mama called from the kitchen. "You go on back to bed now. I'll get the castor oil bottle and turpentine and put it on the stove to get warm."

After the bus rolled up our street, Mama walked down the hall with her castor oil and listened to the silence. We knew we had to go to school every day, no matter what. Nobody stayed home for her medicine. Because of her discipline, not one of her seven boys dropped out of high school.

I was always more afraid of my mother than my father, even though Calvin C. Williams Sr. was easily the biggest man in Winston: six feet four, 270 pounds, For eighteen years Pop had been the man I wanted to become. He had worked hard as a truck driver, a good job for an African American man without a high school diploma, and every Sunday he had sat tall on the front row of our little church while Mama sang in the choir and my brothers and I sat in the back with our friends. He had a good reputation and a little money in his pocket. Pop and my mother were a team, bringing up Stan, Greg, Reginald (everybody calls him "Yogi"), Calvin Jr., Quency, Percy, and me.

In addition to her discipline, Mama gave us an example to live by. She was a missionary in our own community, sharing Christlike love with others who were in greater need than we were. Like when a young woman with a child and a new baby had no husband. The woman hurt her back and could not work, and Mama went to her house to clean and cook. Mama bought groceries with her own money and nursed the mother back to health.

After my brothers and I had grown and left home, Mama had even more time to help others, and she started taking in foster children—more than fifty of them over eight years. She gave each of them the same loving care she had given us, doing those things not through her own strength but through the strength of Christ living through her.

A friend once asked her, "Katie, how did you raise seven sons, and none of them got a girl pregnant and none of them dropped out of high school? How did you do that?"

"I didn't," Mama said. "God did."

The world had given my mother the credit for raising her boys, ministering to neighbors, and taking in neglected children. Yet Mama knew she couldn't do any of those things on her own. Every morning she went to her knees and asked God for guidance, strength, and wisdom. She prayed for each of her seven boys, and she believed in the power of answered prayer. Through her faith, God allowed her to do more than she had ever asked or imagined.

That's the lesson I missed. I went to Auburn as a freshman and became the hardest-working player in the weight room and on the practice field. I learned to rely on my own strength and discipline and had no idea how much I limited myself with my self-reliance. Like the people in Jesus' hometown, I did not put my trust in Him to perform mighty acts. I never allowed God to use me as His instrument, so my physical, mental, and spiritual capabilities ran into brick walls. I began to fail in places where I had previously succeeded. Failure led to frustration, and frustration led to bitterness, and before the end of my second season at Auburn, everything around me had begun to sour.

3

WHEN WE WERE
THE LEAST OF THESE

"When you give to the needy, do not let your left hand know what your right hand is doing, so that your giving may be in secret. Then your Father, who sees what is done in secret, will reward you."

MATTHEW 6:3–4

When we were young, my brothers and I always looked our best on Easter Sunday. Mama saw to that. In March when her tax-refund check arrived in the mail, Pop took half of it, and she used the other half to buy seven Easter suits for her boys.

One year, however, Pop said he was taking the whole check.

"But I need it for the boys' clothes," Mama protested. "They've outgrown everything they have."

"They'll get by," Pop said.

That wouldn't do for Mama. She refused to have her sons looking poor any day of the year, but especially on Easter.

Riding to work the next morning with four co-workers, Mama stayed quiet as she pondered her options. She understood the irony of working in a clothing plant all day, sewing suits she couldn't afford to buy. Mama had started out sewing lapels on jackets. Then, because she was good at the sewing machine, she had been promoted to pockets, which were much more complicated. The owner of the company—everybody called him Mr. Roy—walked through the plant almost every day and inspected the women's work. She knew by his low "um hmm" that he was satisfied with her work. As good as she was, however, Mama only knew lapels and pockets. She couldn't sew an entire suit. She couldn't make our Easter clothes. So she devised a plan for her boys that only a mother would attempt.

The company allowed employees to buy cloth remnants for next to nothing, so Mama picked out her material one day during her break, and she bought seven patterns. During a break the next day, she walked over to Mr. Roy's office. I can only imagine how nervous my mother must have been walking down the hall toward the owner's office. This was the late 1960s, and it was a white man's world. She believed Mr. Roy was a good man, and by attempting this plan she was not risking her job. But getting fired was always a possibility.

His secretary let her in. With only a few minutes before she had to be back on the line, she got right to the point. (In fact, at this point she probably feared her supervisor out on the floor more than the man looking up from behind his desk.)

"Mr. Roy," she said, "I have seven boys, and they always look their best on Easter Sunday. But this year we just don't have the money for new clothes."

"How can I help?" he asked.

"Well, I have the cloth to make suits, but I can't make them. I just do pockets."

He leaned way back in his chair and twirled his pencil around his thumb. He knew what she was asking, and he didn't make her say it out loud. "You got the patterns?" he asked.

"Yes, sir."

He paused again, still thumbing that pencil. "Let me ask you something. If somebody did this for you, who would you tell?"

"Well, I guess I would have to tell my husband, but I wouldn't have to tell anybody else."

Mr. Roy rocked quietly in his chair and looked at something on his desk. "What if somebody did it for you and you didn't tell your husband?"

Mama thought about it and said, "I guess that would be all right."

He was quiet again, and Mama started shifting from one foot to the other. She had to be back on the line in a couple of minutes or her supervisor would send somebody looking for her.

Finally he said, "Bring the material and the patterns to my office tomorrow, set them down inside the door, and keep walking. When they're done I'll call you to my office as you go home, and you take them straight out the door with you."

"Yes, sir," Mama said, and she wanted to hug him. But she couldn't.

He leaned forward, put his elbows on his desk, and looked right at Mama. "This stays between the two of us. Understand?"

Mama wiped the smile off her face. "Yes, sir," she said. "Thank you." Then she turned and hurried out of his office and back to her sewing machine, trying to keep from grinning all the way down the hall.

The next morning Mama brought the material and patterns and did as she was told, and after a few days she saw her material show up on the plant floor. "I don't know who these are for," she overheard a woman who was sewing one of our jackets. "I heard it was something special for Mr. Roy—maybe his grandchildren."

The next afternoon Mama got a message to stop by Mr. Roy's office. On her way home, she walked down that long hallway, looking around to see who might be watching. His secretary had stepped away from her desk, so Mama peeked in his office, grabbed the bundle by the door, and walked quickly toward the exit.

Easter came, and Mama presented our new suits. We had never even gone shopping. Pop asked where she got the money, but she wouldn't tell. He demanded to know, and still she refused.

In fact, Mama might have taken this memory to her grave if my work on this book hadn't led her to remember the many times she had experienced the generosity of others throughout her life.

Only then did I learn that Mr. Roy B. Sewell—one of Auburn University's most generous benefactors and whose name I saw a thousand times on the front of the athletic dorm where Quency and I lived— had been quietly generous with my mother and her seven little boys nearly forty years ago. "I wish I had taken a picture of those suits," Mama said.

Every day I walk across campus and see the names on buildings, streets signs, and sports venues—recognition of the dedication and generosity of those who have preceded us.

Our Lord doesn't see those things. Instead He remembers the unnoticed acts of kindness. "I needed clothes and you clothed me" (Matthew 25:36). Our family was among those Christ described as "the least of these brothers of mine," and Mr. Roy B. Sewell, taking care to do his good work in secret, clothed us in splendid suits to celebrate the day of our risen Lord.

4

THE ELUSIVE BIG TIME

"Whoever wants to become great among you must be your servant."
MARK 10:43

If the love of money is the root of all kinds of evil (1 Timothy 6:10), pride and the love of fame run a close second. The Bible mentions pride dozens of times, usually in a negative light, reminding us that pride run amuck leads to quarrels, destruction, downfall, disgrace. Dr. Martin Luther King Jr. called it the "drum major instinct—a desire to be out front, a desire to lead the parade, a desire to be first. . . . We all want to be important, to surpass others, to achieve distinction, to lead the parade."

When Dr. King delivered that sermon in 1968, I was five years old, and our family was living in a little shack on sixteen acres at the end of the road in Winston, Georgia, about thirty miles due west of Atlanta. We had a well in the backyard and chickens running around under the house. I didn't even know what a drum major was. But those were the happiest days of my young life. I could run for hours through the woods or go hunting with my friends. We killed more songbirds than I want to admit, and my cousin took most of them home for his mother to clean and cook. We played games with pocket knives and sticks. We played Switch, where you had to run around the house and get back to base (the porch) before "It" caught you and wore you out with a switch. Then the state decided to run an interstate highway through our backyard, and they took eleven acres of Pop's land and much of the woods beyond. Then came the fire.

We were sitting down to supper one night when I was seven, and my oldest brother, Stan, went to get an extra chair from the bedroom. With seven boys and two parents, sitting at the dinner table at our house was a game of musical chairs every night—the last one had to go find a chair. Sometimes I ran to the table half-dressed to keep from being last. Before Stan came back with the chair, I was already reaching for a piece of bread. Stan screamed from the other room like a snake had bit him. I dropped the bread, and we all jumped and ran toward the bedroom. He was standing at the door looking in at the ceiling, which was engulfed in flames.

"Get out of here!" Pop yelled, and all nine of us turned and ran toward the kitchen door. Mama grabbed up Percy, who was five, but the rest of us ran empty-handed. Then we gathered in the backyard between the well and the outhouse and watched the flames burst through the roof. Neighbors wandered over to watch with us and listen to the dry wood crack. My baseball and bat were inside. So were Greg's football and all our clothes. I was wearing a pair of green pants. No shoes. We heard the siren in the distance, and somebody asked how it started.

"Don't know," Pop said.

"We'll have to get up some things for you and the boys. Did you get any of your pictures or anything?"

"Nothing," Mama said. "It's all gone."

The heat pushed me back into the crowd of grown-ups.

"We can take one or two of the boys 'til you find something," Uncle Kenny said. He was my father's brother and had walked over from across the road.

"That's good," Pop said. "Chette'll stay with you."

Then others claimed Stan, Greg, Yogi, Calvin Jr., Quency, and Percy. There were no tears and not much emotion. I guess when you don't have a lot to lose, losing everything doesn't hurt as much.

The siren got too loud for us to talk, then the fire engine stopped in front of the house. The firemen climbed out and watched. The house was too far gone to do anything else, and probably wasn't worth saving even if they'd gotten there earlier.

"Let's go," Uncle Kenny said, and we walked across the road to his house. By nightfall somebody had brought me a box filled with clothes and shoes that were close to my size.

I lived with Uncle Kenny for a couple of months. He was a preacher at a church up in Buford and another one down in Barnesville. All of my father's brothers were preachers. Uncle "Bear"—the Rev. J.R. Williams—pastored a church in Bowdon. Uncle A.E., the best of all, moved to Chicago shortly after he was called to preach, and came home years later and pastored Pine Street Baptist Church in Marietta. He retired from there and came home to work with the pastor at Old Mountain Top Baptist, our little stone church in the woods on the outskirts of Winston.

Mama says Old Mountain Top started under a birch arbor before the Civil War. Two birch trees still grow in front of the church. They're covered with resurrection ferns that turn brown and crunchy during dry spells, then spring back to life after a soaking rain. Behind the church a cold spring boils up and runs down into Waterfall Branch. Across the road on the side of Cedar Mountain lies the church cemetery.

Every Sunday, even the month or so when we were split up after the fire, Pop drove us all to church in his Cadillac. Percy and I sat in the front seat between our parents, and our five older brothers crowded in the back, kicking and pushing each other all the way.

At church I sat in the back with my friends, cutting up and laughing, but when the preacher stepped into the pulpit, especially if it was my Uncle A.E., I stopped and listened. I was nine when I started thinking about the preacher's altar calls. My older brothers had gone up front to the altar before, and some of my friends had gone up too. They were all a part of something I didn't quite understand, and I wanted to be a part too. So one Sunday when the preacher came down to the altar, I stood up. I liked the way I felt—kind of light and dizzy—walking up the aisle, and when I got to the front, the preacher asked me some questions about whether I understood what it meant to give my life to Christ. I said I did, and when the hymn ended, he announced that I was committing my life to the Lord and was ready to be baptized. After church the next Sunday we went out back and he took me down to the creek. He dipped me into the water, and I came up knowing that I belonged to something, but I didn't understand what.

My father was a proud and determined man, and as I grew, I developed those same traits. When I was eleven, I saw what it meant to hit the big time, and I knew I wouldn't be living at the edge of the interstate for the rest of my life. That was the year Bear Bryant came to our house. Shug Jordan came too, and so did Vince Dooley. They all sat on our living room sofa and tried to convince my brother Greg to play football for them. Greg was my hero. Coach Jimmy Johnson at Douglas County High School had nicknamed him "Deac," because he played defensive end like Deacon Jones, the Los Angeles Ram defensive end who invented the term *sack*. Greg was six feet three, 210 pounds his senior year, and he was so quick he ripped past offensive tackles before they could come out of their stance. Every college in the South wanted him, and the University of Georgia got him for defensive coordinator Erk Russell's "Junkyard Dawgs."

Greg had his future laid out for him. He had all the physical tools to become a professional football player. But it wouldn't be an easy road physically, mentally, or socially. His fame would come at high personal cost. Ray Goff, who was Georgia's starting quarterback during Greg's freshman and sophomore years, recalled years later, "Public schools had been integrated for a few years, and African Americans were still in the minority—maybe five or eight out of forty scholarships. Then we'd go into places like Oxford, Mississippi, where they were waving all those Rebel flags and hollering things, and it could get tough. It was tough enough for me as a young white boy going to Oxford. I can never know how hard it was for a minority facing that.

"Then you come home to Athens, and if you're a minority in the midseventies playing at the University of Georgia, there's not a lot for you to do. No place to go at night—everybody doing their own thing."

I had no idea what Greg was facing. I was just a kid. All I knew was that Greg was living a dream—playing college football and setting his sights on the NFL.

By his junior year, 1977, Greg was starting at defensive left end. Georgia had a terrible offense that year—seven starters had graduated in 1976—but the Junkyard Dawg defense had allowed only three touchdowns in the first three games of the season against Oregon, Clemson, and South Carolina. On October 1, Georgia traveled to Tuscaloosa to play Alabama.

There was no way any of our family could get over to Tuscaloosa, but Coach Johnson went to the game. When he saw Greg put a vicious hit on All-America fullback Johnny Davis, he knew somebody wasn't getting up. The collision was too violent. After a few seconds Davis stood and walked away. Greg remained flat on the field. Coach Johnson hurried down the aisle and onto the field. Nobody stopped him as he went to Greg, who was conscious but couldn't move. Paramedics brought out a stretcher, and when they put Greg into the ambulance, Coach Johnson climbed in with him and rode to the hospital. He called us from the emergency room to tell us that Greg's neck was broken, but the spinal cord wasn't severed. He was able to move his fingers and toes, and the doctor was already giving him a good chance of complete recovery. But he would never play football again.

Greg wore a neck brace for months. He could have returned to Georgia on scholarship and completed his education, but without football, he had no desire to return. So he came home and tried to make it in Douglas County—another former high school star athlete with no college education, on the street looking for nonexistent opportunities. That was the extent—and the cost—of Greg's fame.

Five years after they recruited Greg, the college coaches came back to our house, this time looking for Quency, who was just a year older than me. We had always called Quency "Tiger," because he was a wild man. When he was little, he chased one of my brothers with an ax, and another time he shot at us with a bow and arrow. He played defense with the same kind of abandon, and, like Greg, he was big—six feet three, 215 pounds.

I was a junior playing noseguard and was even quicker than Quency. In fact, nobody was quicker off the ball than I was, and for most of the season Quency and I took turns as Douglas County High Defensive Player of the Week. But the recruiters hardly noticed me. I hadn't played at all my sophomore year, still recovering from breaking my hip in a playground accident. Now they just wanted to see Quency, who was six inches taller and thirty-five pounds heaver than I was.

I cut the grass in the front yard, and Mama cleaned the house and put supper on to cook before each recruiter showed up at the front door. When they came in, I sat in the living room with them. Quency and I could be a package deal, I believed.

"I've got even more tackles than Quency," I told every recruiter.

"I think we probably have a place for a player like you," the coaches told me, then they turned quickly back to Quency. Ray Goff, who was recruiting for the University of South Carolina, wanted Quency so badly he all but offered a scholarship to me too. He would burn two scholarships to get Quency. Maybe we *could* be a package. Then Quency signed with Auburn, and we never saw another college recruiter at our door. My pride told me they were all wrong, and I was determined to prove myself right. Nothing but the SEC—the big time—would do for me.

5

RECRUITING FOR THE LORD

*We do not know what we ought to pray for, but the Spirit himself
intercedes for us with groans that words cannot express.*

ROMANS 8:26

I had no idea as a teenager that I was being bathed in prayer every day
by both my mother and an assistant football coach. They prayed for
me more than I prayed for myself, and I know now that their interces-
sion changed my life.

Coach Hal Young offered me a ride home from practice one afternoon—Winston was about five miles out from school—and when he
cranked up his pickup truck, Christian music poured out of the ra-
dio—music of praise and power that reinvigorated me after a hard day
of practice. Riding down the highway we talked football, not religion,
and Coach Young convinced me that despite the lack of attention from
college recruiters, I could play Division I-A football. "But you're going
to have to get a lot bigger, faster, and stronger," he said.

Coach Young had been a walk-on football player at Auburn, playing on the freshman team in 1965. But he realized the following spring that the varsity operated at a level he would never achieve, and he left the team to focus on his degree. To play football in the Southeastern Conference, he told me, I would have to strengthen my body. He agreed to work with me in the weight room after school.

In the weight room Coach Young spotted me on the bench press and pushed me on the squat rack. All the while he talked with me about different Bible verses, what they meant, and how we could apply them in our lives. He challenged me to read my Bible every day, and he invited me to a Fellowship of Christian Athletes meeting on a Monday night. Coach Young was the leader of our school's FCA chapter, and every Monday the group met at a different student's house. Sometimes on Sunday nights he took some of the guys to Mount Paran Church of God, where the choir was bigger than the entire congregation of the little church I grew up attending.

Then on Friday afternoons during football season, most of the team crowded into Coach Young's biology classroom for a voluntary prayer meeting. He prayed with us over our injuries and prayed for our families. We shared our personal problems, and he prayed with us about them. What I didn't know then was that one day every week he fasted. He skipped lunch and went alone into the closet adjacent to his room and prayed for an hour, lifting each of us by name.

While Coach Young prayed for us, I prayed for myself. I wanted a football scholarship, but it wasn't happening. Halfway through my senior season, I began to get the picture. By this time a year earlier, Quency had already visited college campuses all over the South and was scheduled for more. This year the telephone hadn't rung. Not once. I knew the recruiters were in the stands, because my cousin Cleve Pounds, who played linebacker and was just a junior, was already getting some notice.

Surely the college coaches could see by the end of the season, after five shutouts, how I had created havoc in offensive backfields all year and could do the same for them. I was quick and strong, bench-pressing 375 pounds and squatting 600, even if I wasn't as big as they liked. Still the telephone sat silent. My only chance was for Douglas County to play deep into the playoffs, maybe even for the state championship, where the stands would be filled with recruiters.

Then Marietta beat us 10–0 in the regional semifinal game, and my football career was over. I began to wonder whether I would work the rest of my life moving furniture or join the military after high school graduation. My prayers had gone unanswered, or so I thought. What I didn't realize was that my mother, Coach Young, and the Holy Spirit were all making intercessions on my behalf, and each of those prayers would be answered.

At the same time, Coach Young had become for me a model of the kind of Christian man I would aspire to. He came alongside me and learned my interests and life goals, then helped me achieve them. He talked openly and easily about Jesus Christ without pushing his theology. He fasted secretly, as Christ admonishes us. And he prayed for me.

6

PUTTING THE TEMPLE ON DISPLAY

*Don't you know that you yourselves are God's temple
and that God's Spirit lives in you?*

1 Corinthians 3:16

Arnold Schwarzenegger came out of retirement to win his seventh Mr. Olympia contest in October 1980. Maybe that's why the skating rink over in Paulding County decided to have its own bodybuilding contest. The owners were always looking for a way to attract a crowd on Sunday nights—dancing with a DJ or dance contests, whatever it took. My friend Harvey Zachery heard they had some professional bodybuilders competing, and he wanted to see what one looked like.

Harvey was a year behind me in high school. He played defensive back, and we spent a lot of time working out together in the weight room. We thought we looked pretty good. "But we're just country boys," Harvey told our dates when we were driving out to the rink. "We just want to be strong so we can take a block or knock a guy off the ball.

We're not like those guys trying to look pretty or sexy. We don't care how we look."

(That last part was a lie. There's not a high school boy alive who doesn't care how he looks. I spent way too much money on clothes and too much time in front of the mirror working on my jheri curl. That's just what we did in 1980.)

"That's right," I said. "Muscles are for function, not for showing off."

My date, Sheryl, snickered, and I didn't say anything else until I had parked the car and we got our skates out of the trunk. We paid our money and went in. The floor was packed with skaters, but we had barely gotten warmed up when they announced the contest.

Melvin, Harvey's brother, waved us over, and we found a place on the floor near the little stage. The announcer explained the rules—the contestants would come up one at a time and go through the seven compulsory poses, beginning with the front double biceps and ending with the front abdominal-thigh isolation.

"What's a front abdominal-thigh isolation?" Harvey's date asked.

"I'll tell you in a minute," he said. The first guy came out wearing a little Speedo and all oiled up. The crowd went wild. The guy stopped right in front of us, sucked in his stomach, and flexed his biceps. More cheers and whistles.

"That's the front double biceps," Harvey said.

"We're sitting too close," I said.

The guy put his hands on his waist and flexed, then he turned to the side, grabbed his left wrist with his right hand, and flexed again.

"Man, you're cut better than that guy," Melvin told me. "You ought to be up there."

"I ain't no bodybuilder," I said, but I knew there was at least one competitor I could beat.

As the first contestant walked off the stage, I stood and said, "Let's move back some so we can stand up."

The other contestants were waiting over to the side, and Melvin said, "Look at those guys, Chette. You could beat every one of them."

"They got nothing on you," Harvey said.

"I said I'm not a bodybuilder," I insisted, but I liked what they were saying, especially in front of our dates.

"He's right," Sheryl said. "You should have entered the contest. You could've won."

"I'll be back," Melvin said. I knew where he was going, and my palms started to sweat.

Melvin came back a minute later and said, "You're in!"

"No way."

"Absolutely. You're in."

"I mean, no way am I getting up there in one of those little bikinis."

"You don't have to," Melvin said. "They said you can wear your pants. Just take off your shirt and shoes."

"You gotta do it, man," Harvey said. "For the country boys."

I looked at Sheryl. She smiled.

"Come on, man," Melvin said. "Let's get you in the bathroom and get pumped up. The lady said she'd put you at the end, but they'll get to you pretty soon."

I started unbuttoning my shirt as Harvey, Melvin, and I cut through the crowd to the back of the rink and into the men's room. The girls waited in the crowd.

"Do some push-ups," Melvin said. "Harvey, go get a towel."

I looked at the tile floor. "Not on the bathroom floor," I protested.

"Okay, then, against the wall."

Somebody on stage was looking really good, because the yelling and whistling echoed against the back wall. This was a bad idea.

I put my hands on the wall and leaned into it. Melvin put his hands against my shoulder blades and pressed hard. "Push!" he said. "Push harder."

After thirty push-ups my triceps were bulging. Melvin burst in. "Here's a towel," he said, "but you better hurry. They just have four left."

"Go find some oil," Melvin told Harvey.

"Aw, come on," I said.

"You saw them guys," Melvin said. "You got to glisten. Harvey, get the oil."

Harvey ran out again. "Curls," Melvin ordered, and he held the towel out. I grabbed it with my right hand and he pulled down hard as I lifted. "Good, man, good," Melvin said. We did thirty curls with each arm, then Harvey pushed back in.

"Got some baby oil. Here."

I squirted some on my hands and started working on my arms and chest. "Get my back," I said, and Harvey rubbed some on. Luckily, nobody came in to use the bathroom.

"Now let's get out of here," Melvin said, and we ran across the rink as the announcer called, "Next up, Chette Williams." I kicked off my shoes, pulled off my socks, and jumped onto the stage, and the crowd clapped politely. Except for one guy in gym shorts, I was the only contestant without a Speedo. I tried to remember what the others had done. The double biceps was easy, and so was the hands-on-the-hips thing. I held it for a minute and stared at the wall at the back of the room. I didn't want to know if people were laughing at me. Melvin and Harvey whistled, and our dates yelled for me, and suddenly the crowd was into it. I didn't remember the next poses, so I just started winging it, flexing, and turning under the lights. I finished and hurried off.

"Give me my shirt," I told Harvey.

"You're not done yet," he said. "There's another round."

"Only if the judges vote me in."

"Are you kidding? You're in, man!"

Sure enough, the announcer called five names for the second round, and I was in.

"You better smile if you want to win," Melvin said.

"Huh?"

"Act like you're having a good time up there."

In the second round they called all five of us on stage at the same time for what they called a "posedown." They cranked up some music, and we all started flexing and turning. I didn't know what to do, so I watched the others and did what they did. One guy looked like a real pro—tan and bulging from his shoulders to his ankles. I took my cue from him. The announcer would point to one of us, the crowd would cheer, and the judges would signal. The guy in gym shorts was still up there, obviously a crowd favorite. They seemed to consider him and me underdogs and got behind us. Finally, the announcer touched the guy in gym shorts on the shoulder and signaled him to step back. Then he touched another and another, and I was standing out front with the pro. It was down to him and me.

They cranked up the music louder. He put both hands behind his head and pulled, and his biceps looked like they would explode out of his skin. Then he put one hand behind his back and pulled again, and his triceps bulged. I tried to do the same poses, but it wasn't working for me. He had practiced too long. I had to do my own thing to win. When he flexed his thighs, I knew I was beat. Melvin must have had the same thought I had, because I heard him yell, "Do it, Chette!" I could take off my pants and still be wearing more than that guy; then we'd be fighting a fair fight. But I couldn't bring myself to do it.

The music drowned out the crowd, and I started moving with it. Then I remembered a move I had done a thousand times in front of the bathroom mirror, one that nobody else in the world had seen me do. I flexed my left pectoral muscle, then my right, left, then right, and they were doing a little dance under the lights. The crowd started clapping to the beat, and I knew I had them. I smiled and flexed my biceps, triceps, and abs all together and kept the rhythm with my pecs. The other guy looked at me and laughed, and the music stopped. It was over.

Then the announcer called, "And the winner is . . ."

I never heard his name. All I knew was I didn't hear "Chette Williams!"

"You was robbed!" Harvey said. "We all was robbed—all the country boys with muscles that matter."

We walked out to the parking lot and my shirt stuck to the baby oil. Second place. Arnold didn't have Chette Williams to worry about.

7

GOD'S GAME PLAN

In the beginning God . . .
GENESIS 1:1

The Bible begins with God, through His Word, bringing order to chaos. At times in our lives, it seems, only God can straighten out the mess we've created, and only in looking back can we see the Spirit of God hovering over the face of the waters, speaking His order into our lives.

In the spring of my senior year in high school, my parents called all the boys home to talk to us. Percy and I were the only ones still living at home. Quency drove up from Auburn, where he was having his own trouble with the new coaching staff, and when Stan, Greg, Yogi, and Calvin Jr. showed up, we all went into the living room. Pop and Mama told us they were getting a divorce, and I didn't understand. After all these years, what could have happened?

They didn't tell us then, but Mama had known for years that Pop wasn't bringing home his entire paycheck. He was sending some of it to other women out on the road to support his other children—my two half sisters by two other women. He had asked Mama for a divorce a year before they called us in, and she had refused. So he stepped up his womanizing to make life completely unbearable for her, and she finally relented.

Mama still talks wistfully about Pop in their younger years. "When I married, I could see myself with a white house with red roses and Calvin and me taking our children to church," she says. "I was in college, and when we married, the witness was the secretary of the probate judge at the courthouse. She said, 'You're going to college, and you're marrying a man with a seventh-grade education?' It should have hit me then, but I was too in love." Mama had all sorts of ambitious plans about businesses Pop might start for their sons to grow in to, but Pop just liked driving that truck.

I hated Pop for his betrayal. He had cheated on Mama and every one of us. He had been our example, our role model all my life, and all along he'd been living a lie. I wanted Mama to fight him—to take the house and everything she could get from him—but she didn't. She just moved out to the little frame house we had lived in for several years after the fire and left Pop in the brick house up on the hill. Before long he was married again, and his new wife was in our house.

High school graduation was coming, and I had no a plan other than to play college football. With no scholarship offer, I found it easier to feel sorry for myself than to develop a backup plan. After school every day I earned money moving furniture for The Brass Bed, and the store manager said I could work full time after graduation.

A few days before graduation Coach Hal Young gave me an FCA

Bible, *God's Game Plan.* He told me he was confident that God had a plan for my life, but I wasn't so sure. He hadn't revealed anything to me. At graduation they called my name and I walked onto the stage to receive my high school diploma, and the next morning I went back to work at The Brass Bed. I could see every day for the rest of my life lined up before me, moving furniture or driving a truck, wondering if I might be better off joining the military. At least they would pay for college.

A week later Coach Johnson called and told me I had been invited to play in the Georgia High School All-Star Football Game in July. One more game. What a gift! All the great players would be there: Robert Lavette and John Dewberry, who were going to Georgia Tech; Knox Culpepper and a bunch of others who were Georgia recruits; and some Auburn guys, including Ben Thomas, Victor Beasley, Ken Hobby, and Ron O'Neal. Their coaches were all coming to watch them play. Maybe somebody would notice me.

I got a week off from work to live and practice at Woodward Academy in College Park, south of Atlanta. Both teams, North and South, stayed at Woodward, and they brought in some of the best high school coaches in the state to work with us. I listened jealously as everybody talked about where they would be playing football in a couple of weeks and what they were doing to get ready. I was one of only two players on campus who did not have a college scholarship. We worked hard for three days in midsummer Georgia steam heat, and on Wednesday, our head coach, Cecil Morris of Duluth High School, told me I would be starting at noseguard. This was my last chance to get that scholarship.

The weather changed on Thursday, and when the sun dropped behind the west stands just before kickoff, the night turned strangely cool after all the hot practices. The South took the opening kickoff, and we took the field on defense. After a couple of stops, they had the ball third and long, and Ken Hobby never had a chance. The most sought-after high school quarterback in Georgia broke the huddle and looked over the defense while his teammates took their positions. For Hobby, who would report to Auburn University in a few days, the Georgia High School All-Star Game was just an exhibition. For me, the game was everything—my last chance.

I took my stance across from the center, a guy from Macon who outweighed me by fifty pounds. My fingers sank into the thick Bermuda grass, and I looked the center in the eye. He was dripping with sweat on the third play of the game. Hobby walked up to the line and started calling signals, and I cheated over a few inches toward the gap between the center and right guard. The center's knuckles turned whiter as he tightened his grip on the ball; then he snapped it to Hobby, and I shot through the gap. The guy barely grazed me, and before Hobby had dropped back two steps for a quick out pass, I was all over him.

The whole game went like that, it seemed. I had three or four sacks and a couple more tackles, and when the clock ran down, I knew I had done my best. Most of the players stayed out on the field while college coaches and recruiters came down from the stands to visit with the guys they had signed. Vince Dooley was there, along with Pat Dye, Bill Curry, and others. I hung out on the field, knowing they had to have seen what I had done and wondering if one game was enough to turn some heads my way. But other than a few people telling me, "Good game," I didn't get much notice.

My size was killing me. I was quick enough to beat any high school center in the state off the ball, but the college coaches were looking for somebody quick *and* big to play defensive lineman. My best game ever hadn't been enough. I held my head high and my shoulders back, and I felt tall as I walked back to the locker room, but inside I was beginning to feel sick. I might have just played my last football game ever, and I didn't have a plan for next week.

The college coaches followed us to the locker room, and I had to watch them talking to their boys. I slowly lifted off my shoulder pads, and somebody behind me said, "Good game, Chette." Hey, somebody knew my name! He introduced himself, said he was Coach Jim Fuller from Jacksonville State University, and he needed a guy just like me for his Gamecocks. He was offering me a scholarship right then and there! Jacksonville State had just built a beautiful athletic complex, said to be the finest in NCAA Division I-AA. But that's not what I wanted. My dream was still Division I A, a major school, the SEC. I told Coach Fuller I would have to talk it over with my parents.

A few minutes later a coach from Troy State University introduced himself and offered me another scholarship. He said I had the kind of game they were looking for. The attention was nice, but I still watched the big name recruits with envy. Dooley was talking with his man Culpepper and a tight end from Gwinnett County, and Curry with Lavette and Dewberry. Coach Dye had come to Auburn from the University of Wyoming in December, when most of the recruiting had been completed, so he had come to the game to see his Georgia boys play for the first time. I was out of the shower and almost dressed when Quency came into the locker room. He looked across the room at me, then walked over to Coach Dye. A minute later they came over to my locker, and I stood up. Quency introduced us, and I learned that Coach Dye was a man of few words.

"Son, I like the way you played tonight."

"Thank you," I said.

"I'm sure you have some scholarship offers—all of mine are committed for this year—but if you come down to Auburn and play the way you played tonight, we'll get you a scholarship next year."

Quency was standing behind him smiling, and I tried to keep from grinning too big. Auburn. *The Southeastern Conference.*

"Yes sir," I said.

That was it. He walked away, and I could have hugged Quency. I had my foot in the door, and that was all I needed. I would get that scholarship and be the third Williams brother to play SEC football. I finished dressing and looked around at the other guys in the locker room one more time before leaving. *Yes, men,* I thought, *I'll be seeing you on the field again.*

Somewhere around midnight I sat on my bed in my mom's little house thinking back over the week, the game, and Coach Pat Dye inviting me to Auburn. I was about to be the sixth boy Mama had sent out into the world, and I had an opportunity to make her proud. I wanted to remember this night and this feeling and make the most of it, so I reached over and pulled a notebook and pen from my books and started writing the goals I would accomplish:

1. GET A COLLEGE DEGREE

Neither of my parents had college degrees. Mama left college when she married Pop. Greg had a chance, even after he broke his neck, to complete his degree at Georgia, but he never did. Stan went straight to the military, and Yogi and Calvin Jr. went to work right out of high school. Quency and I needed to earn our degrees from Auburn and turn things in a new direction for the Williams family.

2. PLAY FOOTBALL

I didn't want to sit on the bench and yell, "It's great to be an Auburn Tiger!" I was quick and strong, and I could work hard and get even stronger. I would be a player.

3. MAKE MAMA PROUD

My mother supported all of us through our sports, but sports weren't so important to her. She encouraged us to finish high school and go to college, but even that wasn't her highest ambition for us. Mama wanted each of us to become a reliable, responsible, trustworthy Christian man. Being the first son to leave home after the divorce, I had to be so good that she would forget about all of that trouble and be proud of her boy. I would bring some order to the chaos of our family.

I looked at the paper and my goals again, then I folded it and slid it into the Psalms, in the middle of *God's Game Plan*, where I would see it every day at Auburn.

8

INTO THE DESERT

Anger resides in the lap of fools.
Ecclesiastes 7:9

My father filled the door frame of the house—his house now—eclipsing the Georgia August sun. "You'll never make it at Auburn," he said. "You're not big enough, and you know it."

I felt my fists clench. *I'll be a bigger man than you.* I caught the words before they spilled out of my mouth.

"You should've taken the offers at Jacksonville or Troy," he said. "Those were real scholarships."

"I told you what Coach Dye said," I told him again. "If I practice hard and play tough, I can get a scholarship at Auburn next year. He liked what he saw last week."

"He just said that to get him another blocking dummy. Look at you! You'll never be big like Greg or Quency. Those boys down there are gonna eat you alive."

"You watch me," I said, and I pushed my way past him out the door.

"You go on then!" he said. "But you'll be back!"

I slammed the door of my green Chevy Laguna and scratched off in the dust, hit the pavement on Post Road, and didn't look back. I cranked up the stereo and let the hot wind blow through the open windows, wondering if Pop was watching me drive away. If the fight had really been over football, we might have walked away mad and come back together after a while. But I wanted to hate my father for his treatment of my mother and now for belittling me. I carried an anger in my heart that the Old Testament writers would say "waxed hot" and would burn for almost two years, leading me into what seemed at times to be a "vast and dreadful desert, that thirsty and waterless land, with its venomous snakes and scorpions" (Deuteronomy 8:15).

From day one at Auburn, I was "Little Q," Quency's little brother. In his freshman year, under Coach Doug Barfield, he had started at defensive end. Then Barfield was fired and Pat Dye was hired. He was a tough disciplinarian. Coach Dye had been an All-America guard at the University of Georgia, served in the army until 1965, and for the next nine years was an assistant coach for Bear Bryant at the University of Alabama. He described himself as "an old horse trainer. I make it easy for players to be right and hard for them to be wrong. We demand certain things from a discipline standpoint."

Some of the players, including Quency, reacted angrily to Coach Dye's brand of discipline, and Quency's actions resulted in punishment and limited his playing time. Out of loyalty to my big brother, I was certain he was being mistreated.

I had my own issues with the coaching staff. My entire freshman year in 1981 I worked at linebacker with the scout team, emulating opposing defenses for our first-team offense in preparation for each game. Every freshman works with the scout team, especially nonscholarship freshmen like me. I didn't like it, and I wanted off. The best way I knew to get off was to show the coaches how tough I was. I wanted Coach Dye, from up on that tower where he watched us, to see me and say, "Hey, get him out of there. He needs to be playing defense."

My pride drove me. Instead of working with the mind-set of helping the team, I went crazy on the practice field, running all out and trying to hurt somebody, if that's what it took to get noticed. And when I cracked Willie Howell's ribs, they noticed.

My downhill slide became a spiral. Not only was I lonely, angry, and frustrated, I was also hanging out with the party crowd. A varsity football player, I learned, doesn't have to look far for a party. Guys are quick to share a beer or a joint, and girls are quick to share as well. I broke curfew and got caught time after time, then I argued with my coaches over the punishment—up and down the stadium steps with a concrete block on my back. I sought relief by getting drunk or high again, but when I came home and closed the door, I was even lonelier and more exhausted than before. I rarely fell into a peaceful sleep.

Then Kyle Collins showed up. Kyle transferred from Jacksonville State University after his freshman year, and his locker was beside mine in the walk-on locker room. I sized up Kyle quickly: redneck country boy from Gadsden who talked too much about God. I expected to see him some afternoon standing at Toomer's Corner handing out tracts. He invited me to FCA, and I said I'd think about it, but I knew I wouldn't. Nobody could do FCA like Hal Young had in high school.

No point getting involved in a second-rate program. Kyle was always trying to make conversation, and I tried hard to ignore him. In fact, I would have run from Kyle if I could have. The good news was, he was a running back, so I didn't have to spend much time with him on the practice field—just in the locker room before and after practice.

Life began to improve in my sophomore year. Despite my bad attitude, Coach Dye gave me the scholarship he had promised. I graduated from the practice squad and got some reps at linebacker. I played even more on special teams, especially the kickoff team busting the wedge, the perfect place for my kamikaze style. The bad news was, they kept recruiting other linebackers and putting them ahead of me in the defense depth chart.

In my frustration I started popping off at the coaches. All the other players told me I should be playing more, and I believed them. Quency still wasn't getting the playing time he deserved either, and I thought he was as good as anybody out there.

My anger grew even as Coach Dye was turning Auburn football into something special in just his second year. With Bo Jackson and Lionel James in the offensive backfield, and the defense shutting down just about everybody, we won six of our first seven games. Still I stayed mad just about all the time, especially on the practice field. A coach told me to give him more effort, and I said he was getting all I had. Coach Wayne Hall might have been the worst of all. He had a way of getting in my face right when I was at my limit, and all I wanted to do was smash him. One afternoon he put his hand on my shoulder, and I knocked it off. We stood toe to toe for a minute until another coach stepped between us just before we started fighting. They kicked me off the travel squad for the Florida game that Saturday, so I decided to go home for the weekend. I grabbed a couple of beers and headed out from campus. Somewhere about fifty miles south of Winston, I hit a little Porsche 914 at a stop sign and knocked it into the car ahead. The Porsche wasn't damaged, but the other car was, so they called the police to investigate. The policeman came and saw that I had been drinking, although I was not over the limit, and he decided to take me in. I had to call somebody to come get me.

I couldn't call Mama and disappoint her, and if I called one of my brothers, Mama would find out. My high school teammates were off at college, so I called Coach Young. He came for me, and I spent Friday night at his house. It was like coming home. Just as God promised, He took a bad situation and turned it into something good. Coach Young and I talked about the Lord in ways I hadn't discussed with anybody in nearly two years. We prayed, and Coach Young read the Bible out loud. He didn't let me off the hook for my behavior. He'd heard about me from Neil Callaway, the line coach at Auburn who was in charge of recruiting in North Georgia. "Coach Callaway says you're becoming a problem on the team. What's up?"

I told him my side of the story, and he listened without interrupting. He just sat quietly and let me hear my own excuses and understand how ridiculous they sounded, even to me. Then we prayed— mainly he prayed for me while I listened.

On Saturday Coach Young took me back to get my car, and I vowed to straighten up. A week later I was back on the field when we beat Rutgers, and the next week we were getting ready to play Georgia, ranked No. 1 in the nation. After practice one afternoon, some of the guys suggested we go out for a drink, and I was in. I came in after curfew, and a few minutes later Coach Daniel knocked on my door.

After Daniel told me I was off the team and left my room, I lay on the bed awhile. Once again, I couldn't call home, and I couldn't tell

Quency. He'd blow up and get himself thrown off the team if he found out. I rolled over on the bed, and on the table beside my bed sat the FCA Bible Coach Young had given me two years earlier. I hadn't opened it at Auburn, even after our talk less than two weeks earlier. I lifted it and held it with both hands, just looking at it and thinking about those good days when he had told us about the promises of God and the comfort of the Holy Spirit. I opened it to find those promises and feel that comfort, but I couldn't remember where to turn. It had been too long.

Then I saw the piece of paper where, on the night of the Georgia High School All-Star Game, I had written my commitment:

Get a College Degree
Play Football
Make Mama Proud

I shut the book on my promises and put it back on the table. "God, where do I go now?" I asked. "Who can I talk to? Who will pray with me?"

None of my party friends would understand how to pray, and I couldn't call Coach Young again less than two weeks after our time together. Who could help me find my way out of this wilderness?

The only person I could think of was Kyle Collins, the FCA guy. I pulled on a shirt and used the front of it to wipe the dust off the Bible, then walked out the door and up two flights of steps to Kyle's room.

9

BRIDGING THE CHASM

Who shall separate us from the love of Christ? Shall tribulation, or distress, or persecution, or famine, or nakedness, or peril, or sword?

ROMANS 8:35 (NKJV)

I knocked on Kyle's door, but he didn't answer. I knocked again, still nothing. So I turned the knob—it was unlocked—and pushed it open. Water was running in the shower, so I stood in the doorway and waited. If I stepped any farther in, he might think I was trying to steal something. His Bible lay open on his bed, and I craned my neck to see what it was open to, but I couldn't. The water turned off, and I stood up straight. Finally he stepped out into the room, then flinched, startled.

"Chette!" he said, then he looked at my Bible. I lifted it a little to confirm for him what I was holding.

"Hey, Kyle."

"What's up? Come in."

I stepped in and pushed the door closed. I had never made small talk with Kyle, and I couldn't think of anything to say now.

"Sit down," he said, and I sat on the empty bed. He sat on his bed, and for what must have been only a couple of minutes but seemed like an hour, the only sound in the room was the air conditioner running. I thought about telling him about Coach Daniel's visit, but I didn't want his sympathy.

Finally I held my Bible toward him. "Will you read to me?" I asked.

"Sure," he said, and he took the Bible and opened it. "What do you want me to read?"

I didn't know. I wanted assurance of what the preacher had told me back home ten years ago when I walked down to the creek behind Old Mountain Top Baptist Church to be baptized. I wanted to know that I could rely on the promises Hal Young had read to me. But I couldn't remember what either man had told me. All I could remember was the feeling I experienced when they spoke God's promises—a feeling of comfort and assurance. I needed that feeling now. I was falling fast, and I needed a rope to grab or a rip cord to pull, or I was going to slam into the earth and be lost forever.

Kyle looked up from the Bible.

"You didn't come here to read, did you?"

"No."

"What's going on?"

I looked at the Bible, still open in his hands. "Coach Daniel said I'm off the team."

"Mm," Kyle said, and I waited for more. The air conditioner whirred for a long time. "Is that why you came here?"

I didn't have an answer. I wasn't sure in that moment why I had come to Kyle's room.

"You came here to make a decision, didn't you?" he asked.

A decision. Yes. I was ready to decide. And I knew which direction Kyle would go.

I nodded.

"You know, Chette, what you're doing here has nothing to do with what Coach Daniel said. This is a matter of the soul. Are you really ready to give your life to God?"

I nodded again and made a sound from down in my chest.

"Before you do, I'm going to ask you, are you really ready to do this? I'm not talking about just being a Christian. I'm talking about making a total commitment to your work in school, to your social life, your dating life, to athletics—I'm talking about totally submitting to the power of God. Because let me tell you something, Chette, if you're not willing to do that, you're wasting my time."

I looked Kyle in the eye and said, "I'm ready." I tried to hold his eye long enough for him to see that I was sincere, that this was as real as anything I had ever experienced. But he was skeptical. He had to be.

"All right," he said. "Understand, now, that there is nothing magical in the words you say. What matters is what you believe."

"Okay."

Kyle slid off the bed and onto his knees on the floor, and I knew he expected me to. I did, and he reached over and took both my hands. He closed his eyes and bowed his head, and I did the same. "God, I know I have sinned and fallen short of your glory," he said, then he paused, waiting. I repeated the prayer. I shivered a bit, and my hands twitched. He continued, "I believe with all my heart that Jesus is your Son, and that He died on the cross so I can be forgiven." Again, I repeated Kyle's prayer, and in my mind I was walking down the hill behind Old Mountain Top Baptist Church toward the creek with the preacher beside me and my parents and brothers all around. I climbed down the bank and stepped into the water. It was colder than I had expected. I wrapped my arms around myself, and the preacher put a hand on my shoulder. He said a prayer thanking God for my eternal salvation, and then he put one hand behind my shoulders, the other over my face, and pushed me down backward into the water. It was freezing. He lifted me up as my cold, heavy clothes clung to me, and I wiped the water off my face. My mother was smiling and waving her hands back and forth like she wanted to clap for me, and I tried to smile. "Father," Kyle said, bringing me back to the present, "I believe that Jesus rose from the dead, and I ask you right now to come into my life and be my personal Lord and Savior. I repent of my sins and will worship you all the days of my life."

I repeated the words, and Kyle let go of my hands. I opened my eyes. Nothing had changed, not Kyle and not his room. There had been no lightning bolts, no hand waving, no tears. Then Kyle said, "Chette, today your name has been written in the Book of Life. You are forever saved from damnation and hell, and you are now eternally with Christ."

I was not sure what that meant. I hadn't come to Kyle running from my eternity—I wanted to turn around in *this* life, and I knew I couldn't stay turned in the right direction without help. Kyle couldn't help me—we lived in two different worlds. We hardly spoke to each other, even now. I didn't know anybody who could help me except Jesus, and I wasn't sure what He could do. I just knew He was my last hope. I stood and picked up my Bible from the bed and walked out the door. I went back to my room, turned on the light, opened my Bible, and began to read.

10

THROUGH KYLE'S EYES

"Who is my neighbor?"

LUKE 10:29

Kyle remembers the night of my salvation:

Chette lockered next to me in the walk-on locker room, and he was not a very desirable guy to hang out with or be around. Somewhere along the way he didn't go to charm school. He was mean looking and a little scary. The Chette Williams from the old days was the total opposite of what he is today. Today he walks into a room and lights up the place. Back then he was mean, angry, and bitter.

I had become a Christian a year and a half before that night and had engaged in a Bible study with some guys. I can't say what compelled me to start praying for Chette. I told the other guys in FCA that I was going to pray for him, and they said, "You've got to be kidding! Come on, you don't need to pray for that guy. He's a lost cause. Pray for somebody you can have some success with."

When Chette stepped in to my room that night, my first thought was, *What's going on here?* I realized what he was asking, and all I tried to do was seize the moment and not screw it up. *Don't say anything wrong*, I told myself. *You've been praying for this for a long time, and now here he is, so don't screw it up.*

I honestly don't remember what I said. My mind was spinning, and I know I didn't offer anything deep—no great spiritual truths.

Then it was done, and he walked out of the room. I sat on the bed in awe of what had transpired, but doubting any lasting change would take place. His reaction had been so weird. Usually there are tears or celebration or some sign of release. With Chette there was nothing. Not even a thank you.

Did he understand what we were saying? Did I? The whole thing had been surreal. I wish I could be more descriptive than that. I had to sit on the bed and ask myself what had really happened. It was as if God had entered the room and taken over our minds and hearts and my mouth. It was not the best sermon I had ever preached and not the most profound thoughts I had ever conveyed. In fact, it was really childlike. As soon as he left the room and I gathered my thoughts, my mind went to all the profound things I should have said.

Why had I been so hard on him when he had come to me for help? Who was I to threaten to turn him away and tell him he might be wasting my time?

Then I started to consider my responsibility. I now had a

bond with a man I hadn't had a relationship with two hours earlier. If he had questions, he was coming to me.

Sure enough, early the next morning I heard a knock at the door. Nobody likes early visitors at the athletic dorm, not even me.

"Who is it?" I asked.

"Chette."

"What's up?"

I sat up in bed. He opened the door, and the guy's face was different. I don't mean it was like Moses when he glowed coming down from the mountaintop, but he had a different countenance. Softer. Relaxed.

"I need to ask you something," he said.

"Sure."

"Can I tell people I'm a Christian?"

It's true! I thought. *Last night really happened! Chette has changed!*

"Absolutely," I said. "In fact, you need to tell people."

At that moment I felt something wretched pushing up from inside of me. I hadn't liked Chette, and I hadn't loved him. I didn't understand him, and I hadn't even tried to understand him. All those months I had reached out to him with my words and prayed for him, but I never expected him to be my friend. We had nothing in common. He was a black man. I had black friends—every athlete in the South does. We are teammates. We stand side by side. We block for each other, run for each other, push each other, and stand beside each other. But Chette was different. He hadn't earned my allegiance. He was a mean, ugly black man, and I was afraid of him.

Then he walked away from my doorway a new man, while the prejudice I had felt for Chette and so many others tore at me like a legion of demons. I prayed to Jesus to cast them out—to forgive me for seeing this man as something less than myself.

Once again, there were no lightning flashes, and I shed no tears. But like Chette, I had turned and was walking in a new direction in a new understanding of Christ's admonition to "love your neighbor as yourself."

11

ONE DAY AT A TIME

Therefore if anyone is in Christ, he is a new creature;
the old things passed away; behold, new things have come.
2 Corinthians 5:17 (NASB)

Morning came. I opened my eyes and wondered what to do next. I was a Christian, and I was no longer an Auburn Tiger. I had to go home, but first I had to apologize. Coach Dye had invited me to Auburn to be part of his team and had given me a chance to earn a scholarship. I responded by becoming a cancer on his program, and now he was cutting me away like "a branch that is thrown away and withers; such branches are picked up, thrown into the fire and burned" (John 15:6).

I dressed quickly and walked up to Kyle's room to see if it would be okay for me to talk about what had happened. He said yes, so I hurried down the hill to the coliseum. I knew Coach Dye would be in his office. He came in early every morning during the season, especially this week with Herschel Walker and the Georgia Bulldogs coming to town on Saturday.

In some ways Coach Pat Dye was bigger than life. He had been cut from the same bolt of cloth as Vince Lombardi, the great Green Bay Packer coach, with his tough discipline and his demand for excellence. Twenty-four years after he removed me from his team, Coach Dye looked back:

> Football is a violent game, and Chette was a violent man—a very aggressive football player. His effort and personality on the football field were exactly what you're looking for. But he had that same personality off the field, and sometimes that's not conducive to getting along. Even so, as a person, he was just as important as the best player we had. I wanted every player on our football team to feel that way.
>
> Chette had a burning desire. He worked hard. The physical part of football was easy for Chette, even though his size was not exactly what you're looking for. Chette wasn't the greatest football player that's ever been. He wasn't a superstar or somebody we couldn't play without.
>
> I might have spent more time with Chette because he needed more time, I don't remember exactly. It might have gotten to the point where I had to spend too much time with him. He was at the end of his rope, and he had to decide if he wanted to be part of the football team or be a hoodlum. Some decisions send you down a dead-end street. It's just a matter of when you get to it. Chette might have reached the dead end.

Coach Dye's door was open, but I knocked anyway and felt an

instant twinge of regret. The top-ranked team in the nation was coming to town in a few days, and he didn't need to be dealing with a troublemaking player. That's why he'd sent Coach Daniel to my door ten hours earlier. I'd have to make it quick.

He looked up. "Good morning, Chette."

"Coach Dye, I want to apologize," I said.

"Come in. Have a seat."

I sat down and told him I was sorry for my behavior and my attitude. I was sorry that he and his coaches had to spend their time worrying about me, and I didn't blame him or anyone but myself for cutting me loose. He leaned back in his chair and listened, nodding slightly but not smiling or speaking. I couldn't tell if he believed me, but couldn't blame him if he didn't. Then I told him about visiting Kyle and my decision to give my life to Christ. My year and a half at Auburn had looked like a total loss, I said, but now a new door had been opened for me.

Saying the words out loud I felt an indescribable lightness, as if Christ was there in the room with me, giving me the words. I held on to the chair to keep from standing up as I talked. Coach Dye looked directly into my eyes the whole time, trying to read me. I never glanced away. I finished and stood to leave, but instead of wishing me well, he said, "Tell you what, Chette. You come on out to practice this afternoon, and let's just take this thing one day at a time."

"What?" I said, and before he could answer, I said, "Uh, sure, great. That's great. Thank you." In an instant I was restored. Just like that, I was an Auburn Tiger again.

And isn't that exactly the way it was with Christ the night before? I had walked into Kyle's room a sinner on my way to hell, and I walked out still a sinner, but restored—saved by Christ in an instant. Now my responsibility was to build a relationship with Christ "one day at a time." The apostle Paul had described it: "Continue to work out your salvation with fear and trembling" (Philippians 2:12). Paul didn't mean that my work would lead to salvation; Christ had already taken care of that. Rather, I must every day exhibit the life of Christ through my words and actions, use the talents He gave me for His Kingdom—to give Him complete reign in my life. Starting right now.

That afternoon I was walking to the coliseum, and Doug Smith drove up in his big Buick Electra, the same one the cops had chased us in.

Doug and I had been showing a big-time recruit around campus and drinking a few beers before practice one day when a police car behind us hit its blue lights. We knew we were in trouble, so Doug hit the gas hard to get away. You can't get into much of a high-speed chase on the Auburn campus, and it was only a minute or two before the cop had us cornered on a dead-end street, jumping out of his car with his pistol pointed at us. We all got out with our hands in the air, and we never saw that recruit again. We laughed about it later, after we had finished running our stadiums.

Now here was Doug, my drinking buddy, with a couple of beers on the front seat, half an hour before we had to be at practice. I knew he would laugh when I told him I couldn't go with him, and I was tempted to lie and make up some excuse. But I didn't.

"I gave my life to the Lord last night," I said. "I can't go with you."

I waited for him to say something like, "Well, I'll give it a couple of days and try you again," but he didn't. Instead, he said, "Chette, I really respect that. I've been trying to do that all my life."

I've never heard more encouraging words, and as Doug drove away, I walked two feet off the ground across the parking lot to the coliseum.

Here's one more story of my transformation, told by another teammate, Todd Burkhalter, that might help show what God did in my life.
Todd had been leading the Bible study group that Kyle was in.

One day Chette and I were the last two people in the locker
room, and I felt compelled to speak to him. I was a little afraid of
Chette, even though I was bigger than he was, but I told myself
to be bold. He wasn't acknowledging that I was even in the room,
so I said, "Chette." He looked up with that grimace he wore every
day, and I said, "I just want you to know that we've been praying for
you in our Bible study. I want you to know that God loves you."

With that, he somehow looked even angrier, and he said,
"How do you know God loves me?"

He threw down something he'd been holding and walked
out of the locker room. I was afraid he was going to get his brother
Quency, who was just as mean as Chette and a lot bigger, and
they would come back to beat the snot out of me, so I got dressed
faster than I had ever dressed in my life and got out of there
before they came back.

In retrospect, I believe the Holy Spirit was already beginning
to prevail upon Chette because of our prayers. He was struggling,
wrestling, and the whole thing was coming to an apex.

A few days later I saw Chette in the first-floor hallway at
Sewell Hall, and he started running toward me. I froze, because I
thought this was going to be the death blow. But as he came
closer, I realized he was smiling. Really smiling. Then he embraced
me and said, "Todd, I've become a Christian!" I couldn't believe
it. Chette had undergone the most dramatic change I have ever
seen. He was a new man.

12

SEEKING COMFORT
IN THE DEATH OF A TEAMMATE

I will dwell in the house of the LORD forever.

PSALM 23:6

More than once I caught myself speeding whenever I drove my Laguna back to Auburn. The roads were empty on that warm Saturday morning in August 1983, and I was pushing hard to get back to campus, even to face two-a-days and three weeks of practice before the first game of my junior year. This was our year. My year.

Preseason polls ranked Auburn fourth in the country, highest in twelve years, and our schedule—we called it our "Road to the Top"—included four top-ten teams. I had emerged from spring drills second on the depth chart at linebacker, and I had a chance to make a real impact on our success.

I had also vowed to become bolder in my Christian witness. Since Kyle had led me to Christ, I had felt the Holy Spirit energize me whenever I stood in front of a group and told my story. But I still found it hard to talk to friends one-on-one. I remembered how I disliked Kyle's bold approach before my own conversion—how he had been the kind of guy I would run from—and I didn't want to appear like that to others. I could talk to strangers about my faith, but not my old drinking buddies. I had to find a way.

I pulled into the Sewell Hall parking lot and started hauling my things into the room. Some of the other Georgia boys were coming in at the same time. Lionel James and Greg Pratt rode over from Albany, Ron O'Neal from Atlanta, and Jim Bone from Columbus. We hadn't given ourselves time to catch up—we had the first part of our physical exams down on the baseball field right away. We hustled over to the locker rooms in the coliseum to change clothes, then hurried to the field.

I was already soaked with sweat when I stepped onto the grass. It must have been ninety-five degrees. This part of the physical required us to run four 440-yard laps. The coaches added an element of peer pressure by grouping us to run by position. If any player didn't beat the required time, all of the players in his group had to run again.

The linebackers, defensive ends, and fullbacks ran as a group. We had to finish each lap in under eighty seconds—not a sprint, but more than an easy jog. With a ninety-second break between laps, the test gave us nearly ten minutes to run a mile—not a problem for most college athletes. But we worried about Greg Pratt, who had made our group re-run a couple of laps the year before. Greg was one of our hardest-hitting, hardest-working players, and he had earned the starting position at fullback. He would be blocking in the wishbone offense for our star halfbacks, Lionel and Bo. At five feet eight, 235 pounds, he was as strong as our offensive linemen, but he struggled with his stamina, and his off-season training wasn't the most rigorous.

The coach blew his whistle, and Greg lit out like he had something to prove. I paced myself and stayed back as Greg finished the first lap in first place. Winded, he took a knee for his ninety-second break, then jumped up for his second lap. He didn't win this time, but he finished in the pack with me, then he put both hands on his knees and tried to catch his breath. Sweat was pouring off of him, and the rest of us encouraged him to stand up and get some air. The next two laps would be tough for Greg, and we didn't want to run extras. One of the managers brought him some water, and he poured it over his head to cool down.

We lined up again, and I stepped over close to him. "Let's go, man. You can do it. Just an easy jog in the park." The whistle blew and we started. Several of us stuck with Greg and let him set the pace. Around the outfield we ran so slowly we could talk the whole way. "Pick it up a little. A little faster and we'll make it."

"I know," Greg gasped. "I know." He was leaning forward, his feet pounding the grass with every step.

"You can do it, man. You can do it," one of the guys said, and Greg straightened up for the last hundred yards. We made it, and he flopped down on his back. Just one more time around and we'd be done. But I couldn't see how Greg would finish in time. Then ten seconds before the whistle blew for us to start again, he stood up, breathed deep, and poured another cup of water over his head. "Okay," he said. The whistle blew, and we were off.

We started out jogging—a pace I thought might get us around in time. Then every step came slower than the one before it. Halfway around the outfield fence we were practically walking. "We gotta help him," somebody said, "or we'll be out here running all day." So two of us slid under Greg's arms, and we were able to jog with him, but we weren't going to get there.

"I can do it," Greg said as we turned for home, but we were already over the eighty-second limit. We'd be running again, but Greg wouldn't. Not today, anyway. I wondered if he would be able to play if he didn't pass this part of the physical, or if he would run it again later in the week after he had worked out for a few days. We carried him across the finish line, then we all collapsed together.

Greg didn't get up until the team trainer, Herb Waldrop, helped him up, took him over to the fence, and sprayed him with water to cool him down. When I looked again, Coach Waldrop was helping Greg make his way to the coliseum.

The linemen had finished their laps and we were all walking back to the locker room when we heard the distant whine of an ambulance. It grew louder and louder until it drowned out every other sound, then it was silent. It had stopped at the back door of the coliseum. They were coming for Greg. We ran across the parking lot, and the running backs, who had finished early, said Coach Waldrop was doing CPR on Greg.

I went to the training room to find Coach Waldrop, but he wasn't there. Other players were milling around the hallways looking for anybody with answers. Finally Coach Dye came in and told us to wait in the meeting room; he'd find out and get us some answers. As we dressed, we knew we couldn't just wait. We decided to drive to the hospital and find out for ourselves.

Half the team was standing in the emergency room waiting area when I walked in. Nobody knew anything about Greg. Kyle gathered a group of us together, and we knelt and prayed, but it was almost impossible to see God when all I could see was Greg's face.

Then Coach Dye came in and told us all to go back to campus. He would stay until he knew something, then come and tell us. This time we followed his order and went back to the meeting room at Sewell Hall. Guys who never showed that kind of emotion—Donnie Humphrey, Doug Smith, my brother—were all crying. And when Coach Dye walked in an hour later, exhausted, eyes red, we knew Greg was gone. He said the words out loud, and then one by one, we left in silence to deal with the grief in our own ways.

I don't remember much about our first week of practice. Nobody mentioned our "Road to the Top" schedule. We were just trying to get by. On Thursday the whole team rode over to Albany for Greg's funeral. Hundreds of people squeezed into every seat of the church, lined the walls, and spilled out into the yard. Coach Dye stood in the pulpit and remembered Greg as "a man who no challenge was too big for, no goal unattainable." Then Greg's high school principal said he was "a legend we should nurture and cherish. We should instill in our youth the same virtues he had."

Throughout the service I prayed for Greg, and I continued to pray for him every morning and every night. I felt guilty even as I prayed, because for a year and a half Greg and I had partied together and played together. But since my conversion, I had never talked to him about Christ. I had never prayed *with* him, only *for* him. Like a missed tackle in a game, I prayed that someone else had picked up after my mistake—and that Christ, in His infinite grace, had received my friend. And I vowed never to let another friend go to his grave without having an opportunity to know about Jesus.

For years I didn't receive any assurance in my prayer for Greg. Then as we were researching for this book, I read an interview Lionel

James had given *Inside the Auburn Tigers* magazine. When he talked about the 1983 season, he recalled that hot August day:

> "It was uncharacteristic of Greg to be in the front of his group during those drills," James remembers, "but he was out in front on the first lap. Then he started to lag behind, and by the time it was over, the other guys were carrying him across the finish line. He made it into the dressing room, and I found him lying on the floor of the shower, praying to himself, the Lord's Prayer and the 23rd Psalm. I went over and helped him out of the shower, and he said, 'Tell Mama I'll be all right.' I thought he was okay, and Bo and I went to eat lunch. When we came back, everybody was down on the floor, praying, and Kyle Collins said to me, 'I don't think Greg's going to make it.' I couldn't believe it. I didn't think twenty-year-old athletes could die."

The words jumped off the page, Greg's last words of assurance for himself and all who loved him: "Yea, though I walk through the valley of the shadow of death, I will fear no evil: for thou art with me. . . . Surely goodness and mercy shall follow me all the days of my life: and I will dwell in the house of the LORD forever."

Amen.

13

RESTORING THE YEARS

Restore to me the joy of your salvation
And grant me a willing spirit, to sustain me.
PSALM 51:12

The first weekend after my conversion had been the open date before the Alabama football game, and Todd Burkhalter had invited some other players and me to go home with him. You have to realize, now, that Todd was the guy who one week earlier had said he was literally afraid of me, and now he was inviting me to his parents' house.

In many ways I felt like the old Chette—the person I had been in high school, friendly, optimistic, and desiring a relationship with Christ—was emerging from underneath a ton of garbage and ashes. Except this was better. Christ assured me that this was everlasting. I never had to turn back to the ash heap. Todd's family had a piano, and we sang praise songs deep into the night on Saturday, and on Sunday morning his little country church welcomed us like long-lost brothers.

The next week Coach Dye let me travel to Birmingham, where we beat Alabama for the first time in ten years, and then a week before Christmas we went to Orlando and beat Boston College in the Tangerine Bowl.

During the off-season Todd led a Bible study for players and, through FCA, he offered opportunities for me to tell my story in public. When he asked me to share my testimony at the weekly FCA meeting, I couldn't wait to stand in front of a group and tell what Christ had done for me. I wanted my drinking buddies to hear it too, and even though they weren't excited about coming to an FCA meeting, three of them showed up and sat together. There must have been 150 athletes in the room. Todd invited me to the front and introduced me, and I told them how Christ had changed my life. Then I started talking to my three friends. "This means I won't be drinking or smoking with you anymore, guys," I said, "and I won't be riding over to Tuskegee with you to meet girls." They were squirming in their seats because I was looking right at them, but I wanted the commitment on the record. I wanted all those athletes in the room to hold me accountable for my decision. I was sick and tired of being sick and tired, and I was ready to claim God's promise through the prophet Joel:

"So I will restore to you the years that
    the swarming locust has eaten . . .
You shall eat in plenty and be satisfied,
And praise the name of the LORD your God,
Who has dealt wondrously with you."
    —Joel 2:25–26

A few weeks later Todd arranged for a bunch of us to speak at his little Methodist Church in Leeds, Alabama. I was more nervous this time, but Todd said I wouldn't have to talk about theology or the Bible—just tell my story. We got there, and when the preacher called me up, I told the people who I had been, what God had done in my life, and who I was now. When the service ended, a woman came up to me and asked me to pray for her daughter who was pregnant. Another asked me to lay hands on her. It was a strange and moving experience, but it showed me firsthand a truth I would read later: You don't have to be eloquent, or even educated, to be effective as long as you allow the Holy Spirit to use you. "When they saw the courage of Peter and John and realized that they were unschooled, ordinary men, they were astonished" (Acts 4:13).

Later we spoke at a church in Muscle Shoals, and as the preacher was giving the benediction at the end of the service, a young girl stepped out from her pew and walked up the aisle to receive Christ. She was so bold. God had called her then and there, and she responded the only way she knew how. In the thrill of that moment, knowing that something I had said had triggered a change in a person's life, I couldn't wait to speak again. Riding back to Auburn the guys said the girl's boldness reminded them of me. "For God did not give us a spirit of timidity, but a spirit of power, of love and of self-discipline" (2 Timothy 1:7).

Football started again—my junior year at Auburn, 1983—and with it came the tragedy of losing Greg Pratt. We dedicated the season to his memory and finished the regular season 10–1 with a chance for the national championship if we could beat Michigan in the Sugar Bowl. We did, 9–7, but the win wasn't impressive enough for the Associated Press poll. We finished second behind Miami.

I continued to play a limited role as a junior, primarily on special teams, but a year later in the Auburn preseason media guide, linebacker coach Frank Orgel said, "Chette provides a lot of the intangibles on our team. He is a leader and contributes in a lot of areas." We finished my senior season with an 8–4 record and went to Memphis for the Liberty Bowl, where Bo Jackson scored two touchdowns and we beat Arkansas 21–15.

After the game the Liberty Bowl chairman presented the trophy to the team. Standing beside him, Coach Dye looked out at the players and then at me. "Chette, come up here," he said, and he asked me to receive the trophy for the team.

Why me instead of Bo, who was the game's Most Valuable Player, or any of the five seniors who were All-SEC that year? I wasn't even a starter, yet Coach Dye had asked me to receive the trophy. Years later Coach Dye reflected on that moment: "Chette might have had further to come than any of the rest of them. When you have somebody who overcomes more odds, and you know the struggles they've been through, naturally you have a bigger spot in your heart for somebody like that than for somebody it comes easy to. It doesn't mean you don't love the rest of them. I love every one of them like my children. But if that one makes it, you have a special feeling for him."

Christ had transformed a "bad seed" into a player whom coaches now considered "a leader." The years that the swarming locust had eaten had, indeed, been restored.

14

CHANGING SEASONS

There is a time for everything,
And a season for every activity under heaven:
A time to be born and a time to die,
A time to plant and a time to uproot.

I was not a football player.

For the first time since somewhere back in elementary school, I walked to class in January knowing I would never again strap on a helmet and pads. I was no longer a student-athlete. Just a student. And if I ever went back to the weight room or ran another mile, it would be for myself, not for the team. I missed it already in a way I couldn't explain if anybody asked me to. I was finished, and yet my work felt incomplete.

I cut through the pine trees behind Sewell Hall down the hill behind the baseball field. The morning was cold, in the thirties, but at least the outfield fence cut the breeze. Nothing in the cloudy sky or the damp cold reminded me of that ninety-five-degree August after-noon seventeen months earlier, and yet as I walked past the field where Greg Pratt collapsed, he filled my thoughts. All had been anticipation that day. Greg would be starting at fullback, blocking for Lionel and Bo. Then it was over, and Auburn football had gone on without him.

Two seasons. Twenty wins. Five losses. Didn't even slow down. Now it would go on without me, still winning and losing.

In class I sat at my desk trying to listen to the professor when someone knocked on the door and stuck his head in. It was a student who worked in the athletic department, a young guy. I knew the face but didn't remember his name. The professor stopped talking and looked over. "I need to get Chette Williams," the student said.

What does he want with me? I wondered.

The professor looked skeptical, like somebody was trying to get out of his class. "Williams?" he said.

"Yes, Chette," he said and nodded toward me. "It's an emergency."

Emergency? I closed my notebook and stuck my pen in my pocket.

"Mr. Williams?" the professor asked.

"Yes, sir."

"You're excused for the day." I was already standing up. "We'll see you back here on Monday morning."

"Yes, sir."

The kid from the athletic department pulled the door shut behind me. "What is it?" I asked. "What's up?"

"It's your brother. He's sick. In the hospital."

"Which brother?"

"I don't know. Not Quency. He called. Said it's real bad. Intensive care."

Stan. It had to be Stan. He had done something to himself. Hurt himself. I ran down the hall and left the kid behind, then down the stairs two at a time, the last five in a final leap. "Don't do that, Chette," I remembered Mama calling. "You're too little to be playing like that with those big boys."

I was four years old and running through the house with my five older brothers. Stan had started it. He was eleven and already weighed 150 pounds. He sprinted through the kitchen and out the back door. The stoop was missing, and Stan jumped, landing in the mud halfway across the backyard. Then Greg ran. He was just ten, but he outjumped Stan by more than two feet. Yogi, Calvin Jr., and Quency all ran and jumped, then it was my turn. Mama said stop, but I was already accelerating, my little bare feet slapping the linoleum. I hit the threshold and jumped, flying like Superman, then landed chest first. My head slammed and the shock of it ran down my spine. I heard myself screaming, then one of my brothers rolled me over. I opened my eyes and they were all standing over me, looking down like a huddle until Mama broke in and lifted me up. My blood was on her shoulder. She stepped up into the kitchen and held a towel against my forehead—"Get some ice!" she yelled—then she held me close in her lap. The pain was sharp on my forehead. I knew it must be a bad cut. She took the bloody towel off, put some ice in it, then put it back. I screamed and Mama held me tighter. "You're gonna be all right, little boy. You're gonna be all right."

I reached up and touched the scar as I sprinted past Jordan-Hare Stadium, cold and silent, then up the street to the coliseum, past Pat Sullivan's Heisman Trophy, and into the athletic department. "Use the phone in the first office," the receptionist said before I could ask. I stopped at the door to catch my breath, then put my books on the desk and called. Quency answered.

"Hey, it's Chette," I said.

"It's Stan, man. You better get up here."

"What is it? What's he done?"

"Don't know. Some kind of poison. Just get up here."

"Poison? How?"

"I don't know. Just get up here now."

"All right, I'm coming."

I left my books on the desk and ran out and up the hill to my car. Poison. Had to be a mistake. Stan was crazy but he wouldn't take poison. I got in the car and sped toward the highway.

The night had been closing in on Stan for years. He graduated from high school in 1973 and enlisted in the military; then they sent him home, and he started drinking. After a few years, he started making up stories, crazy stuff, telling people he was the CEO of a company. Stan knew something was wrong, so he saw a doctor. After that, when he was on his medication, he acted normal. We knew when he was off it, because we got calls at home. He'd yell at somebody because they didn't respect his position, and Pop would have to apologize and explain that Stan was confused. People were afraid of Stan because he was six feet five, 320 pounds.

I was home from Auburn one weekend my freshman year when Stan came in telling Yogi and me about the company he owned.

"Shut up," Yogi said. "You don't own any company."

Stan kept on; it was obvious he believed it himself.

"Man, you're crazy," I yelled getting up from the sofa. "Why don't you take your pills and straighten up!"

"You're the crazy one if you don't show me some respect!" he yelled back, and he started for me.

Yogi jumped on him, then I jumped on him, and we were beating him—literally trying to beat the hell out of him. He would have killed either of us fighting alone, but together we had a chance. Satan, or a demon, or something, had a hold on him, and we were going to knock it out. We rolled on the floor swinging and kicking until Stan grabbed a telephone receiver and started swinging it, landing it against the back of my head. I fell to the floor, and he shook off Yogi, and instead of coming back at us, he stood up, turned, and walked away like a tired old grizzly bear.

I pushed the back of my head against the headrest and felt the knot that had never gone away. I was driving ninety up Post Road, and I tried to remember how I got there. I slowed at the last curve before the house and saw everybody coming out to the cars. I stopped on the road. "Follow us to the hospital," Mama said. Pop was with them. His wife wasn't.

Six brothers and Mama followed Pop into the hospital and down the hall, following the signs to the intensive care unit. I lagged back with Yogi.

"What happened?" I asked.

Calvin Jr. had brought home cleaning solvent from his job at a chemical plant. He was rebuilding an engine and using the solvent to clean the parts. The stuff was clear as water and had a sweet, fruity smell, and apparently Stan had found it and thought Calvin had some kind of homemade liquor. If he had drunk a glass straight up, it would have killed him immediately. But he had been sipping it for some time, and it slowly ate away at his organs.

"Oh, God, why?" I asked.

We were at the nurses' station, and they said it would be a few minutes before anybody could go in, and then only a few at a time.

"We have to pray," I said.

"That's right," Mama said.

You think you know what to say, then in the emotion of the moment, words fade away. My oldest brother was on the other side of the door passing into the darkest night of his life. "Out of the depths I have cried to You, O LORD; Lord hear my voice! Let your ears be attentive to the voice of my supplications." Stan didn't know Psalm 130, but I believe that was his cry. Like me, he had stood at the altar of Old Mountain Top Baptist Church as a boy and made a decision to follow to Christ, and like me, he had walked down to the cold, spring-fed creek to be baptized. Now he stood at the precipice relying on the grace he had accepted so many years ago. "If You, LORD, should mark iniquities, O LORD, who could stand? But there is forgiveness with You" (Psalm 130:3–4 NKJV).

The nurse called my parents in to see Stan, and when they came back out, Pop was holding Mama up. I wanted to help her, but I had to see Stan. I walked past the nurses' station, and when I stepped into the room, the sickening sweet smell of solvent almost knocked me down. Stan had been exhaling that stuff and filling the room with it. I put my hand over my nose and inhaled slowly as I stepped closer to him. He was massive—somehow bigger than ever propped up with that white sheet pulled up to his chest. His eyes were closed and a ventilator was forcing air into his lungs. He had tubes running out his nose and mouth and I.V. needles in both arms. I knew I couldn't stay long without getting sick, so I just touched his arm and said, "He's coming, brother. He's coming." I prayed quickly for God's comfort for Stan and for us—I was still breathing through my hand—then I left.

Old Mountain Top Baptist couldn't hold all the people who came to say good-bye to Stan. The overflow stood at the front door as the family arrived. So many familiar faces and many more I didn't know. Stan had friends from Atlanta to Carrollton. And there was one white face. Kyle Collins, my spiritual brother, had driven up from Auburn to hug my neck, and I began to understand what it meant to be a real Christian—to go to an unfamiliar place and sit among strangers to show your love.

We carried Stan across the road to the cemetery on the hillside overlooking the church, the spring, and the creek. Mama cried, and my brothers and Pop and I watched Pastor Weldon commit Stan to the Lord's eternal care. After the funeral we went back to the house, where the dining room table was piled high with food from our neighbors. The house filled up with friends and family, and we tried to laugh and let the love we shared overwhelm our sorrow. But a man is not supposed to die at thirty. He is not supposed to be so troubled in this life that he seeks comfort in poison and finds peace only in the life to come. I prayed silently for Stan, my parents, and my brothers. I wanted to speak an encouraging word. For two years I had taken every opportunity to speak at FCA events or to youth groups about God's grace—to share the gospel message. "A time to be silent and a time to speak" (Ecclesiastes 3:7). Now was the time to speak, but in the wake of my brother's death, I couldn't bring myself to say those things to the people I loved most. Not even the 23rd Psalm. I was just Chette, the little boy who had grown up among them. Why would they believe me now? So I stayed silent, and I drove back to Auburn empty and hollow, knowing I had let God down and vowing not to let it happen again.

15

TIME TO GIVE IT ALL

He went out, not knowing where he was going.

Hebrews 11:8 (NKJV)

Follow Me. Over and over I heard Christ's admonition. Every time I opened my Bible, there it was, spoken to Peter and Andrew, then to James and John, to Matthew and later to the rich young man, to crowds and to individuals, and in His final conversation with Peter, the risen Christ told His disciple once again, "Follow Me."

In a few months I would be graduating from Auburn, with no plans for my future, and every time I prayed for guidance I heard the same response: *Follow Me.*

"Follow You where?" I prayed.

Don't worry about where, came the response. *Just follow Me.*

I didn't worry. In fact, I couldn't think of anything more exciting than following Christ without knowing where He might lead. When

Jesus called His disciples, they dropped their nets, left their boats, and followed Him without question. At twenty-two, my nets were filled with nothing but potential, and I was ready to give it all to Him.

I loved to talk to people about Jesus, and I wanted to be in ministry, but I didn't even know what that meant. I needed a starting point, and the only one I knew was back home at Old Mountain Top Baptist, the little church in the woods, where my three uncles all had served as pastor. I asked Pastor Weldon, and he said I could help out as a minister to young adults. In fact, he made me associate pastor and said I could preach occasionally. That sounded perfect except, as I expected, there wasn't much money involved. All of the pastors back home, including my uncles when they had preached, worked regular jobs during the week and preached on Sundays.

I moved back to Winston and rented the basement from Pop, then started looking for a job. Within a few days I was a substitute teacher at Alexander High School and a part-time sales associate at Ellis Men's Clothing Store in Douglasville. Neither of those jobs offered much permanent financial support, but they paid the rent. The apostle Paul became my model as I balanced work and ministry.

On Sunday mornings I spent most of the service in the pulpit, making announcements, reading Scripture—everything except preaching. After a few weeks Pastor Weldon told me I could deliver the sermon on a Sunday morning, and I spent a month crafting my words, praying, and studying. Whenever I thought I had the right topic, I took it before the Lord and asked if I was on track. Finally I settled on a title, "Hot or Cold," and a text, Revelation 3:15–16:

> I know your deeds, that you are neither cold nor hot. I wish you were either one or the other! So, because you are lukewarm—neither hot nor cold—I am about to spit you out of my mouth.

I asked friends from Auburn and Douglas County to support me with their prayers and to come if they could. When the appointed Sunday morning arrived, the church was filled with people who had known me at my hot and cold best and worst: Auburn teammates who had seen my hot anger, former drinking buddies who had watched me turn a cold shoulder to the Lord, new brothers and sisters in Christ who saw the growing fire in my heart.

The service began and I sat in a chair behind the pulpit looking out at all the people who loved me. Pop sat big and tall on the front row. Mama was behind me in the choir. I could smell my brand-new black robe and feel the same nervous tension I had experienced on opening kickoffs before I delivered that first hard lick. Then I stepped into the pulpit and opened the Bible to the text, and in that moment I was flying downfield, the ball sailing high ahead of me end over end toward the return man. The energy of the Holy Spirit poured through me, and I was at total peace. I was home.

I think I had known even before I left Auburn that the Lord was calling me to full-time ministry—not just a Sunday morning commitment. I just couldn't bring myself to take that step. Then a man with a plumbing-parts distributorship in Douglasville invited me to enroll in his company's training program, which would allow me to get my own distributorship. At the end of my training, he said, I could open a store in downtown Atlanta. It was a great financial opportunity, and I entered the program.

Monday through Friday I learned about faucets and fittings and fixtures, then at night I came home to Pop's basement and wrestled with God's call. I never heard an audible voice, but time and time again I experienced a knowing that the Lord wanted me full time. *Follow Me.*

I still wasn't sure what that meant, and when I told Mama what I was experiencing, she said, "If you're going to preach, then you're going to get an education first. I won't have any jackleg preacher for a son."

Her words were harsh, and she didn't mean disrespect to those part-time preachers who had answered God's call. But we both knew my limitations. I had already begun to hear my sermons more critically. Too often they lacked depth, and I didn't know enough to understand what I was missing. I was nearing the end of my ability without more formal training. No lukewarm commitment would do. I had to give it all to Christ. I had to follow Him, not having any idea where He might lead.

I didn't know anything about seminaries—I wasn't even sure what a seminary did—so I called Reverend Bob Baggett, pastor at Opelika First Baptist Church near Auburn and chaplain of the Auburn football team. He suggested New Orleans Baptist Theological Seminary, and when I drove down and stepped onto the campus, built forty years earlier on a large pecan orchard, I felt the peace of the Holy Spirit. This was the place I was being called to.

I had no money for seminary when I left the world of plumbing and had to work on campus for a year to earn enough to begin classes. My first job was on the buildings and grounds, but soon I was undergoing the same training as the New Orleans police so I could be a security guard on campus. Following the Lord's leading was going to be even more exciting than I had imagined.

16

SCARS OF THE WOUNDED

The Lord has anointed me to preach good news to the poor.
He has sent me to bind up the brokenhearted,
to proclaim freedom for the captives
and release from darkness for the prisoners
ISAIAH 61:1

I stood at the seminary gate and looked across Gentilly Boulevard at the "Ice House," a corner known all over New Orleans for its active drug traffic. At two in the morning it must have been eighty degrees, and I was sweating in my uniform. Two women wearing high heels and short, tight skirts stood under the streetlight smoking cigarettes and ignoring me when a black Camaro rolled to a stop and they walked over. One of the women stuck her head in the passenger-side window; the other glared over the windshield at me. Then the driver looked my way, rolled up his window, and hit the gas hard, scratching off when he hit second gear. Now the women were staring at me, daring me to say something. I could feel my pistol, a .40-caliber Beretta semiautomatic, pressing against the outside of my right leg. I folded my arms to keep from touching it. Then I turned and walked back toward the center of campus.

The Sermon on the Mount was becoming real for me in New Orleans, where sidewalks were populated with the poor in spirit and those who mourned—the brokenhearted people for whom Christ announced His blessing. At the same time I was tempted to pronounce an Old Testament-style prophetic message of destruction whenever I ventured downtown, where every doorway and every window spilled lewdness, prostitution, alcohol, drugs, and gambling. The Lord had led me to attend seminary at New Orleans Baptist Theological Seminary, and there I studied under some of the best professors anywhere. But my preparation for ministry occurred mostly outside the classroom among the people of the city.

Five nights a week I wore a uniform and strapped on a pistol to patrol the eighty-seven-acre seminary campus from just before midnight until daybreak. The income paid my way through school. On Wednesday and Sunday nights at 6 o'clock, I went downtown with Clay Corvin, a vice president at the seminary, to the Brantley Center, one of the largest homeless shelters in the country. The center, on Magazine Street a block from the French Quarter, offered supper to people staying the night, sometimes more than two hundred. As I sat alongside the men and women—many of them filthy and smelling of the street, some fighting drug and alcohol addiction, others mentally disturbed—I began to understand what Jesus meant when he said, "Do you love me? . . . Feed my sheep" (John 21:17). God had called me into ministry to preach the Word. But before I could say anything to these brothers and sisters about Christ, I had to love them, sit with them, listen to them, feed them. Loving them was loving Christ.

They were not timid about showing their scars. I learned that many of the homeless were working people—day laborers who didn't earn enough money to pay rent. Each of them had a story to tell. I met a lawyer who had lost his practice, his home, his family, everything to drugs. He was a living embodiment of Genesis 3:19: "For dust you are and to dust you will return." Yet hope remained alive and brought him to the Brantley Center. His hope inspired me and proved the truth of Henri Nouwen's statement, "In our woundedness, we can become a source of life for others."

When the night came that I was asked to lead the chapel service after dinner, the Spirit of God moved in me, and I felt freer than I had ever felt in a pulpit. These people didn't want a traditional sermon. They just wanted to hear truth. I can't tell you the specifics of what I preached because I don't remember the words. I just remember the feeling of the Holy Spirit moving freely and having its way. Over the weeks and months, I saw things I never knew happened outside the pages of the Bible: demons cast out and addictions miraculously cured, lives and families transformed and restored. Every time I brought the message, at least one listener stepped forward to receive Christ. These people had reached bottom, and they had nowhere else to turn.

Still others had not come to be set free; they just wanted a hot meal and a cot, and they walked out the door no different from when they came in. But each of them changed me, even the hecklers in the congregation who were angry or drunk or high.

One Wednesday night I was about to step into the pulpit at the Brantley Center, and I could feel somebody looking at me. I glanced across the room and saw him. *I know that guy*, I thought. Our eyes locked, but his expression didn't change. He just stared, squinting hard. *Oh no*, I thought, *not Demetrius. God, please tell me it hasn't gotten him too.*

College athletes don't expect to see their teammates dying before they turn thirty, but a cloud of death hung over this man. Maybe it wasn't Demetrius. After all, I hadn't seen him in over ten years, when he was driving around Auburn in his yellow Trans Am, smacking running backs on the practice field, and getting a bunch of playing time as a freshman linebacker. He had disappeared after his freshman year, and now I couldn't remember where or why. If this was Demetrius, crack cocaine was draining the life out of him. His brown skin was still taut, but dry and scaly, and in another year or two, after he lost whatever muscle tone he still had, his skin would take on the texture of an old tire. It always does. Finally he smiled a little, and I recognized the gold star in his front tooth. "Demetrius?" I said.

"Wha's up, Chette?" and his right arm raised in slow motion as he reached out to me.

"Man, what's up with you?" I asked.

"Trouble, man. I need help."

"Come sit down and tell me about it," I said.

Demetrius mixed so many lies into his story and left out so many incriminating facts, there's no point trying to retell it here. I know about the lies because he later told me the truth. You see, after he walked out of the Brantley Center for the last time—and we had met several times over the course of a few weeks—he disappeared again. Like so many of the people who came to the center, Demetrius was beyond my help. Only God could reach him now. I could talk to him, preach to him, pray with him, give him lunch money, and try to show him the love of Jesus, but God would have to do a miraculous work to save him from his own choices.

In 2006 as I worked on this book, I reflected on the important moments of my life and remembered seeing Demetrius at the shelter.

Would he still be alive? With a little help I found Demetrius in the Alabama prison system. He is serving thirty years for causing a wreck that killed two people in a high-speed police chase in 1999, and unless he is paroled, he will be sixty-six years old when he is released in 2029.

On a September Monday morning I drove to Staton Correctional Facility to see him. The flat land north of Montgomery is all farm country until you get to the prison sitting like a fenced-in warehouse out in the fields. I turned into the parking lot and wondered why I was here. Demetrius and I hadn't been particularly close as teammates, but that chance encounter in New Orleans had left its mark. Had God brought us together there? Why did God want me here now? Was it simply to visit Him in prison (see Matthew 25:36)? I turned off the engine and prayed that God would allow His will—whatever that was— to emerge in our time together.

I walked across the parking lot and through the first gate and signed in, then a guard led me through another gate and three prison doors to a paneled room. Another guard brought in Demetrius wearing a white prisoner's uniform.

He looked like the man I had known at Auburn, except the gold star was gone from his tooth and he had a long scar across his left cheek. The cloud I had seen in New Orleans was gone. "That was somebody else," he said, smiling and laughing easily, surprised to see me and wondering why I had come.

"Just to see you," I said, "and to see how you're doing."

"I'm doing great, Chette," he said. "God has given me my life back."

"Tell me," I said, and for the next two hours I listened.

Demetrius's early life had been eerily similar to mine. Listening, I recalled something Coach Dye had said about me when he forced me to make a decision: "You had to decide if you wanted to be part of the football team or be a hoodlum."

Demetrius faced the same decision.

Like me, Demetrius had six brothers; he was the youngest, I was number six in our family. In 1981 his father had passed away. That was the same year my parents divorced and I disavowed my father. In 1982 Coach Daniel knocked on Demetrius's door just as he had knocked on mine. Instead of kicking Demetrius off the team, Coach Daniel gave Demetrius one more chance, but he couldn't live in the athletic dorm anymore.

This is where our stories diverged. When Coach Daniel left my room, I turned to a friend who led me to Christ and changed my life that very night. Demetrius thought his punishment was too extreme for the transgression, so instead of taking his discipline, he left Auburn for Grambling State University in Louisiana. He didn't play much there, however, and soon he was back home in Birmingham trying to figure out where he fit in.

This is the critical moment that college coaches and support staff spend four or five years preparing young men to face—the moment they are no longer football players. They try to prepare their players mentally, physically, and spiritually for the rest of their lives. The world tells Division I athletes they can have everything they want—fame, money, women—and the lust for those worldly pleasures led Demetrius down a destructive path. When he took off his pads for the last time, he was lost.

"I started smoking dope and running with some old teammates and some guys that played at Alabama," he said. "I was still working out, and I went to pro football tryouts hoping to land on somebody's program. But out of a hundred guys, they might grab one or two. I needed a friend going in the right direction."

Then one night his mother bailed him out of jail, and on the way home Demetrius told her to drop him off on 16th Street. "Baby, won't you just come home?" his mother asked.

"I got something I need to do." He needed money, and the only way he knew to get it was selling crack cocaine. So he stood at the corner and waited. Soon a pickup truck with two white men circled the block a couple of times. White men cruising that neighborhood at that time of night meant one of two things to Demetrius—they were either buying dope or selling it. The truck came around again, slowed, and Demetrius walked toward it. Then the window lowered slowly and a shotgun barrel emerged. Demetrius tried to run as one of the men yelled, "You (n-word) ain't worth sh--!" Then came the blast, and he was hit in five places in the stomach and right arm.

The incident made the TV news and newspapers because the same men had shot and killed another African American man two nights earlier. Demetrius was scheduled to testify against one of the men when he skipped town for New Orleans. The man was convicted of murder, and Demetrius used the time to rethink his life.

"The Brantley Center was good for me," he said. "It gave me opportunities to get myself back together spiritually and mentally." But the lust for money gripped him tightly, and soon he was selling crack on the streets of New Orleans. He drove to Miami, bought his own stuff, then sold it himself on his own corner. His fortune grew, and after a while he had three kilograms to sell. The first time he hired someone to help him, he got double-crossed and was shot. When he got out of the hospital, he spent ten months in the New Orleans jail.

"Fear drove me back into the Word of God while I was in jail," he told me, "and over time I cleaned up my actions and my conversation."

Back on the street, however, his lust for money once again overwhelmed his jail-cell conversion. Trusting nobody, he went back to buying and selling crack, and when he had saved $100,000, he decided to quit the business and move to New York City. He leased an apartment two blocks from Wall Street and blew through his money so quickly, he had to generate some fast cash. "Like a dog returns to his vomit," Demetrius says, quoting Proverbs 26. "I went back to the same thing."

Then one of his brothers called from Birmingham to tell him their mother had died. Demetrius came home to help bury her, and at the same time he thought he would share his good fortune with his old friends. So he packed a pound of cocaine.

The day before the funeral he was speeding on a Birmingham street when a police car started chasing him. The crack was on the backseat and a crack pipe was on the front seat. Demetrius stomped the accelerator and started throwing things out the window. He was reaching into the backseat when he ran a red light and slammed into a car, killing the couple inside. He cried as he stood before the judge, apologized, pled guilty, and received his thirty-year sentence.

In prison Demetrius has turned back to God. He quotes Scripture easily and prays with confidence. Our time was about up when he touched the long scar across the left side of his face. "My first cut," he said. "A man broke a bottle and cut me a long time ago back home. Before I got in trouble. I nursed that scar for a long time. And every time I looked at myself in the mirror, I thought of you, Chette."

Me? I thought. *Why me? You hardly knew me.*

"It reminded me of that scar on your face," he continued. "I thought about you and how you looked when I first saw you."

I pushed back from the table a little. Why would he have remembered my scar? It wasn't anything compared to the one he was touching.

And mine was from an accident, not a fight. Demetrius and I might have had something in common twenty-five years ago when we were at Auburn, but he's made a lifetime's worth of bad decisions since then.

He didn't stop. "I thought you'd be the one in prison. I'm telling you, man, I was afraid of you. Now look at you. You're a preacher. You've got a sense of humor. I wouldn't have believed it!"

He laughed, and I tried to, but my mouth wouldn't smile. He told one more story that I didn't hear because I kept thinking about what he had said. "*I wouldn't have believed it.*"

He finished his story, and we prayed together. I walked back out into the clear fall morning, and I touched the side of my left eye. I got into my truck and glanced in the mirror. My first cut. Perhaps I had more in common with Demetrius than I wanted to admit.

We're all wounded. We're all scarred, even our Lord. Maybe that's why He led me to New Orleans, and why He led me to seek out Demetrius in a prison. Maybe He was showing me that if I'm going to be a source of life for others through my woundedness, I have to be willing to show my scars.

17

SINGING A NEW SONG IN UNISON

We were all baptized by one Spirit into one body—whether Jews or
Greeks, slave or free—and we were all given the one Spirit to drink.
1 Corinthians 12:13

My mother remembers when I invited a white boy on my recreation league football team to spend the night at our house. The boy's father came to practice every day in a big black car and stood off to the side, and Mama figured he must be rich. The first time the man ever spoke to her, he said his son was looking forward to staying with us. "He said it in such a way," Mama recalls, "that I knew he expected us to have him overnight no matter what I might have thought. The boy really wanted to come."

The father needn't have worried. Even in the early 1970s when many would have felt uncomfortable in that situation, Mama took it in stride. She might have seen black and white, but she didn't want us to know it.

You would think the incident would be burned in my memory. I don't remember it—probably because having white friends spend the night at our house wasn't all that unusual. Since I was a little boy in the early days of integration in Douglas County, I have felt comfortable among people of different races. Six days before I was born, Dr. Martin Luther King Jr. declared his dream of racial reconciliation from the steps of the Lincoln Memorial. I grew into an understanding that his dream would never come to fruition until individuals made it so.

Twenty years after that little white boy spent the night at our house, I was a seminarian in New Orleans. Cottage Hill Baptist Church in Mobile called me to help them start a church where black and white, rich and poor would worship side by side. By helping fulfill their dream, I believed I would also be doing my part to usher in God's Kingdom.

I drove over to Mobile every Friday afternoon, and on Saturday mornings I saw more homeless men and women in one place than I had ever seen anywhere outside of New Orleans. As associate pastor I helped create a Saturday morning feeding ministry for the homeless and invited them to worship with us on Sunday. Then on Sunday a hundred members from Cottage Hill came downtown and worshiped with the down-and-out at the church they were starting, New Song Community Church. The president of Integrity Music became involved and helped us generate the finest praise music anywhere.

As in New Orleans, the Holy Spirit worked in the hearts of individuals. Within days of his first breakfast with us, Byron Beard gave his life to Christ, and a few weeks later Byron and I were serving the Lord side by side. God lit a fire in the soul of this once-homeless man, and the flame spread quickly. Byron knew the people on the street because he was one of them, and when he invited them to church, they came.

God was fulfilling the vision, and the church grew quickly, both in numbers and in depth. I met literally hundreds of homeless men and women who came and ate with us—some I had met earlier at the Brantley Center in New Orleans—and worshiping with them on Sunday morning became a life-changing experience for all of us.

"I have a dream that . . . one day right down in Alabama little black boys and black girls will be able to join hands with little white boys and white girls as sisters and brothers."

We were on our way.

18

GOD'S PLANS

The steps of a man are established by the LORD,
And He delights in his way.
PSALM 37:23 (NASB)

One of the clearest teaching moments in the New Testament occurs when a father begs Jesus, if He can, to heal his son. Jesus, recognizing the man's lack of faith, seizes on the word *if* and puts the responsibility for healing back on the father by telling him, "Everything is possible for him who believes."

The father, who would do anything to help his son, responds, "I do believe; help my unbelief."

Isn't that the challenge for all of us—to believe? To trust God's promise to take care of us and to give us hope and a future?

When I accepted God's call to preach, the decision was easy. There was no downside. Nothing to lose. In the fall of 1995, however, the choice wasn't so clear. Two years earlier the Southern Baptist Convention had called me to New Covenant Community Church in the Algiers neighborhood of New Orleans. Neighbors had started New Covenant in 1985 in an apartment. We moved to an empty storefront in a shopping center with housing projects on two sides and an elementary school across the way. Five or six men from the neighborhood helped me transform the space into a worship center, and when we weren't hammering and sawing, we were going door to door to invite people to worship with us. Walking those streets I invited everybody I saw to come to New Covenant, the moms, the guys hanging out on the street corner, everybody.

So many kids were selling drugs in that neighborhood. Mothers with nothing but a government check sent their twelve-year-old sons out to take care of the family. We created an after-school program with donated computers for the kids, and we tried to reach the families. We counseled women out of abusive relationships and kids off the street. Before long we had filled our space on Sunday morning, and when the store behind us went out of business, we leased that space and knocked down the wall to get everybody in. We borrowed a portable baptismal font from the local Baptist association, and we baptized somebody almost every week. I can't say I've never been happier, but I was very excited about my ministry. Then Dr. Don Wilton called.

Dr. Wilton had been my professor of evangelistic preaching in seminary. In 1993 he responded to the call to pastor First Baptist Church in Spartanburg, South Carolina, where he found a congregation that was reaching into the community. Now, two years later, he wanted to establish an inner-city ministry. To do that most effectively, he wanted an African American minister on staff, and he asked me to become minister of evangelism.

That Dr. Wilton would call me in the first place was extremely flattering. He had been one of my most effective professors and one of the best preachers I had ever known. What he was proposing was nothing short of historic: I would be the first African American minister at the church. Yet I didn't want to leave New Orleans. I had never felt more in line with God's will than I had been over the last two years.

I prayed. For days and nights I prayed about the call, and I asked my friend Bruce Kirk to pray with me. In time I began to experience a peace, feeling that God was leading me to this new place, so I called Dr. Wilton and accepted the offer. Then I called U-Haul and arranged to rent a truck big enough to hold my furniture and pull my car behind it.

About the same time a friend called and said she had a young lady she wanted me to meet, a senior at Southern University. On Halloween night I drove to Baton Rouge and had dinner with Lakeba Hibbler at Outback's. As soon as we met, I was done. She was the woman God had chosen for me. Yet here I was with all of my belongings packed in a U-Haul trailer about to move to South Carolina. Was I doing the right thing?

I thought about Lakeba the entire drive to Spartanburg and vowed to make a long-distance relationship work. Surely God was in our coming together. If the suggestion to meet her had come a week later, we never would have met.

Twelve hours after leaving New Orleans I drove into downtown Spartanburg on a quiet Main Street and saw the big red-brick church at the far end of town. I pulled into the parking lot and got out and stretched, then walked into a side door that led to the gym, where a basketball game was going on. Now, there is a feeling I wish I could describe—a feeling every black person in America has experienced when walking into a certain place with only white people. It's something about the way one or two of the people stop what they're doing and look at you—not in a threatening way, but in a way that makes the one being looked at wish he could step into the first elevator and get out of there right now. I had that feeling walking into that church gym, and all I wanted was to be back in New Orleans.

Then I saw Dr. Wilton jump up from a group in the bleachers and hurry toward me, He made a couple of quick introductions, then asked me to go with Stewart Smith, a young minister on staff and my host until I could find an apartment. Dr. Wilton's demeanor didn't fill me with confidence, and I was beginning to realize that this "historic opportunity" might be more difficult than I had anticipated.

At dinner that night he told me it was even worse. "Chette," he said, "I think I've jumped the gun. Some people in our church are not ready for a black minister on staff." That didn't surprise me; there are always a few people who resist change. But he said it with such sadness, he appeared to have lost a battle either with some in his congregation or with himself. Then he told me he would have to withdraw his offer to me.

Despite his candor and his obvious embarrassment in that moment, I felt no sympathy for him. *Why can't you just tell them to get ready?* I thought. *This is 1995, after all, not 1965.* But I didn't challenge him. Instead, I posed my questions to God, who had brought me to this place and now had me sitting out on a limb with no job, no friends, and no place to live. Not only that, I had left behind a congregation who loved me and needed me, and I had just met the love of my life— back there.

"Why did you bring us up out of Egypt to make us and our children and livestock die of thirst?"
—Exodus 17:3

Like the Israelites, in my fear, anger, and frustration, I lost sight of God's promise.

After dinner Don took me back to Stewart's apartment, and Stewart and I talked and prayed deep into the night. He said several members at First Baptist were committed to the idea of an urban ministry, and they had the financial capacity to make it happen. With the right leadership, they might be willing to set up a nonprofit organization outside the auspices of the church.

Within a couple of days I was meeting with businessmen who had a burden and a passion for reaching out to children in Spartanburg but no avenue to reach them. They told me that my arrival in the city was an answer to their prayer. Soon we had put together a plan for what would become Impact Ministries. Caz McCaslin, recreation director at the church and founder of a ministry called Upward Basketball, helped us see the vision and served on our board. Don Wilton also joined the board, allowing me to focus on forgiveness as we worked together.

We created a Saturday morning program called Super Saturday Sunday School. With vans we borrowed from churches around the city, we brought in kids from most of the twelve housing projects for an hour of games and another hour of Bible study. The next summer we started Acres of Diamonds, a weeklong summer camp for children.

All the while I was calling Lakeba Hibbler back at Southern University and courting her long distance. I invited her to Spartanburg for her spring break, and she stayed with a friend of mine for the week. It was the third time I had ever seen her, and I knew I couldn't let her get away. "Are you ready?" I asked one night when we were out. "Ready for what?" she said. "To get married!" I said. "Yeah!" she said.

We were married in July, and she immediately started helping with the ministry, especially Acres of Diamonds. We drew the name of the camp from the story by Russell Conwell of a poor man who sold his farm and went in search of a diamond mine so he could become rich. It turned out that underneath the fields of the farm he had sold were buried acres of diamonds. In the spirit of the story, we knew that many children in our community could not afford to attend the beautiful summer camps in the mountains around Spartanburg, so we created a camp for these diamonds in our own backyard.

One of the brightest gems we discovered was Samie Clowney. Samie lived with his parents in a public housing project, where he had witnessed drug deals, a shooting right outside his front door, and stray bullets through his living room window. At age thirteen he had committed his life to Christ and was determined to stand up for what he believed in. That commitment often meant alienation from his peers because of his choices. But he never lost their respect. In fact, he was elected president of his senior class. Samie was a junior in high school when I was invited to lead a Bible study at the church his family attended. He introduced himself and shook my hand firmly, and the fire in his eyes looked like the Holy Spirit. I invited him to help with Super Saturday Sunday School, and the children loved him. He recalls:

> I knew all the kids in our community. I grew up with them, went to school with them, and understood them. Chette knew I could identify with kids in their situation, the ones he hoped to reach. That's one reason he wanted me in his program—he knew I was "one of the least of these." At times my family had no food to eat, the lights were about to be turned off, we had no transportation. I knew where to get drugs, where there was prostitution, where to find alcohol. I had seen the guy shoot at our front door and heard the helicopters overhead. I said, "God, you have to get me

out of here," and He sent Chette to let me know that the ministry was a way for me to get out and then come back to serve.

I hired Samie, and we worked side by side in the community even as he enrolled at Wofford College through a scholarship program that required more community involvement. In fact, in his senior year a newspaper column described him as "A Young Male Mother Theresa," adding, "The life of this lovable person is striking evidence of the existence of God."

Samie still believes that God sent me to Spartanburg to offer him an opportunity to minister to others. I know, however, that God sent me there and pulled the rug out from under me so I could learn what it really means to trust His plans—plans to prosper and not to harm, plans to give hope and a future.

19

LOOSE THE BONDS

*Remember how the L*ORD *your God led you all the way in the desert these forty years, to humble you and to test you in order to know what was in your heart.*

DEUTERONOMY 8:2

*R*emember . . .

Remember when your mother fed you beans and cornbread because that's all she had in the pantry.

Remember the frustration of practicing on the scout team day after endless day and the alienation you felt from your coaches.

Remember the night of your salvation and the morning that followed, when Coach Dye invited you to stay on the team.

Remember the SEC championship and the three straight bowl-game wins.

Remember the love you experienced from the least and the lost in New Orleans, Mobile, and Spartanburg.

Remember how God ordered your steps when you thought you had lost your way.

Remember how the Lord your God led you all the way . . .

The telephone rang in the spring of 1999, and when I answered, so many memories came flooding back. Tommy Tuberville, the new head football coach at Auburn, said he had heard about me from John Gibbons, FCA state director for Alabama. (John had been talking with my friend Kyle Collins just a couple of weeks earlier, and Kyle had told him about our ministry.) After a little small talk, Coach Tuberville got down to business. "I've got my offensive coordinator and my defensive coordinator," he said, "and I'm looking for a spiritual coordinator."

Wow, I thought, and I may have said it out loud. *What a commitment. What an opportunity!*

He explained that when he was head coach at Ole Miss, he had a full-time FCA chaplain, Wes Yeary, who worked with all the varsity athletes on campus. At Auburn he wanted a chaplain committed exclusively to the football players. As far as he knew, no other college football team in the country had its own chaplain, but he was already contacting Auburn supporters to fund the position. Would I be interested?

Absolutely.

The team was just starting spring practice, and he invited me to come down and meet the players and coaches and to speak to them as a group for a few minutes. I accepted his invitation, and when I hung up the phone I called, "Lakeba!" I told her everything, and we talked about how hard it would be to leave Spartanburg. As in New Orleans, God was blessing our work, bringing hundreds of children into His program. Was God calling us to leave this? Is this what He had pre-pared us for? In that instant, nothing felt more right to me. Like a compass pointing north, something in me always pointed toward Auburn and told me I would be back someday. "Here's what we need to do," I told Lakeba. "I'll go to the bathroom and start praying. You go to the bedroom and start packing."

I didn't know much about what was going on with Auburn foot-ball at the time. South Carolina media didn't spend much time or ink covering Auburn, and I only knew the basics of the 1998 season: the team started out 1–5, Terry Bowden resigned on a Friday night in the middle of the season, Bill Oliver finished the year as interim head coach, and Tommy Tuberville was hired a week after the Alabama game. The only teams Auburn had beaten in 1998 were Ole Miss, Louisiana Tech, and Central Florida, and now their new coach was the one guy whose team Auburn seniors had beaten every year. What could I tell them?

I drove down on an April morning, and they were practicing in Jordan-Hare Stadium, where we had won twenty games and lost five in Coach Dye's first four years. Coach Tuberville introduced me to his staff. I knew only one of them, Joe Whitt, and I didn't have fond memo-ries of him. He had come to Auburn with Coach Dye eighteen years earlier and had helped rebuild the football program Dye's way. I re-membered the casualties of that difficult transition—young men who had lived and learned in a more relaxed environment suddenly found themselves trapped in a tough, disciplined program. I wondered how many of the players I was meeting now would find themselves in the same position.

At the end of practice, Coach Tuberville called everybody together, introduced me, and asked me to say a few words. The guys were exhausted, and the last thing they wanted was a sermon. So I told them a short story about trained elephants, the strongest mammals on land, yet who can be held in place by a small rope tied to their back leg and a stake in the ground.

"When the elephant is young," I said, "trainers use a heavy chain and a post to hold him, and no matter how hard he tries, he can't pull away. After a while his resistance breaks; then for the rest of the elephant's life, the trainer uses a small rope and a little stake. The elephant *believes* he can't pull away, even though he could quite easily, and he just stands there.

"We can all be trapped by our beliefs, which grow from our experiences, and by the strongholds of the world," I said. "God wants us to cast off the ropes that limit us so we can become everything he has designed us to be."

Remember . . . and then be prepared to forget. "Free yourself from the chains on your neck" (Isaiah 52:2).

I didn't know if Coach Tuberville was interviewing anybody else for the position, but the peace God gave me convinced me as I drove away from Auburn that He had given this job to me. I prayed all the way home and began to think about what I would do. There would be no job description. Nobody had done it before. I would have to rely on God and my own experience.

I remembered the Auburn team I had joined eighteen years earlier. They had lost every SEC game the year before, and then Pat Dye turned the program on its head. What had the players needed through that transition? What would I want if I were playing today? Somebody to listen. A place to vent my frustrations. Somebody to understand what I was experiencing.

These guys needed somebody to cry with them and pray with them, to lift them when they fell face-first, exhausted. They needed to know that God had a plan for their lives. In fact, that would be our theme:

"For I know the plans I have for you," declares the LORD, "plans to prosper you and not to harm you, plans to give you hope and a future."
—Jeremiah 29:11

I would have to earn the right to be heard by the players and to help them discover that plan. They would be skeptical and wonder what made me different from the coaches—why they should talk with me. The answer would come only with time. I would be in the workout room with them before dawn and on the practice field with them after dark. When opportunities arose, I would have to trust God to give me the right word to say, or keep quiet.

I might have to let a player experience pain and let God do His work instead of rushing in and trying to be a savior with just the right word. God has a purpose for our difficult times, and I might get in the way by jumping in and saying, "I have the answer! This is a great opportunity for us to grow together as a family!" A bad experience is not necessarily an opportunity to hit somebody over the head with Jesus.

Remember . . .

Remember who you are and Who led you to this place, God was telling me. *Remember I have a plan for you and for every player and coach, every trainer and doctor, every graduate assistant and manager, every secretary and administrator in this organization. Remember you are a chaplain, not a coach. Coaches spend hours breaking down film and devising ways to win football games. You spend hours on your knees, and I will show you how I win souls.*

20

A NEW DAY DAWNING

I praise you because I am fearfully and wonderfully made.

PSALM 139:14

Ben Leard dropped back and lofted a perfect spiral deep toward the right sideline. Ronney Daniels, running full speed through a thin, rising fog, somehow accelerated to another level, gliding toward the ball and letting it fall lightly into his outstretched right hand as easily as he would pick a ripe pear.

For the first time in fifteen years, I was at a varsity football practice—the first time ever as a sideline observer—and I was struck by the beauty of these athletes' skills. Damon Duvall stood on the ten-yard line and punted a cannon shot to Markeith Cooper standing on the opposite twenty. Tim Castro sprang from a three-point stance and slammed into a blocking dummy with a thud I heard fifty yards away.

The early morning atmosphere, the God-given talent of these 120 young athletes, and the precise minute-by-minute schedule made this first practice of 1999 seem almost as if we had returned to the harmony of the Creation. The first whistle had blown at 5:45 a.m. under the lights of the intramural field, where whiffs of fog had drifted in overnight from a nearby creek. The sky had slowly lightened from black to gray as the players stretched and warmed up, and by the time the defensive and offensive teams had gone to work with their position coaches, the pine trees across the way were silhouetted in rose and light orange. If the Lord still enjoys walking in the garden in the cool of the day, this was the time, before the sun rose above the pines. By 9 o'clock the sun would have burned off the mist and evaporated the dew, braising it with Bermuda grass and sweat in a steamy stew that is unique to football fields on summer mornings in the South.

Two towers rose high above the field, and cameramen up there videotaped practice for review by the coaches. They reminded me of Coach Dye, who always stood on a tower to watch practice, coming down only when a player needed additional motivation. I wondered if practice these days would be as intense as those had been. Coach Tuberville walked back and forth between the offense and defense, stopping to shake hands and talk with three retired men who had walked over shortly after sunrise. "Up mighty early," he said. "I'm Tommy Tuberville."

"We know," one of the men said, and they introduced themselves.

"Find the ball! Find the ball!" an assistant coach yelled from the offensive drills across the field. "*Find the g-- d--- ball!*" Instinctively I turned toward the voice as the words jammed in my ear and twisted in my gut. It's not unusual to hear college coaches using vulgarities and profanities on the field. I heard them every day as a player, and I had no reason to expect this coaching staff to be any different in that regard. Still, I can never get used to the sound of the Lord's name in vain echoing over the east Alabama countryside at daybreak. Or any time of day.

I walked over toward the offense to watch—not to hold anybody accountable but just to see how the running backs looked. Of all the challenges the new coaches faced, this one might be the greatest. A year earlier Auburn had finished 108th in the nation in rushing, and now the team had lost its two leading rushers to graduation and academic trouble. Among our returning running backs, Heath Evans had led the way in 1998 with thirty-six yards for the season. I wondered if Coach Tuberville and his running backs coach, Eddie Gran, looked longingly over their shoulders toward Ole Miss, where Deuce McAllister as a sophomore had single-handedly gained fifty yards more than the entire 1998 Auburn team. Our success this year would rely in large part on the coaches' ability to make the most of these untested athletes.

The beauty of the morning was lost the moment I came alongside the backs as Coach Gran spewed an unprintable shower of profanity. Did he think that kind of tirade would motivate these guys? I wanted to call him aside and talk to him and tell him I didn't think that style of coaching would work. I didn't realize then that God was already in the process of doing just that. Without knowing it, I was watching a man being crushed. Eddie tells his story from the perspective of seven years:

> I didn't know how to control my language. I thought swearing like a sailor and cussing and beating down young men was the only way to motivate them and get what we needed to get out of them. Then I brought that intensity home, and my kids would

hear me swear. It was bad. Really bad.

My wife, Rosemary, was expecting our third child when we arrived at Auburn. We already had two beautiful daughters, Hannah and Dillan, and then on July 1, six weeks before fall practice started, Sydney was born with holoprosencephaly, a rare disease that caused her brain to stop developing during her first three months in the womb. We took her to Children's Hospital in Birmingham, expecting doctors to lead us to a cure. Instead, they told us that Sydney would live for only a few weeks. She would never talk or walk or play with her sisters. In fact, she would struggle to stay alive every day of her short life.

About the time practice started, she started having trouble with her nose. If we put her down, she would quickly turn blue. We had to hold her upright constantly just so she could breathe. Our practice day began before six in the morning, and we reviewed practice films every night until nearly midnight. Rosemary was spending every minute of her time with Sydney just to keep her alive, and at night we took turns sleeping in a chair with her in our lap. Sometimes in the middle of the day, I had to leave to help Rosemary or Sydney, and Coach Tub said, "You take care of them first."

But it was our first year, and our opening game was a couple of weeks away. Our own expectations were so high, and we put tremendous pressure on ourselves.

I dealt with the pressure the way I always had—with my own inner strength. I didn't realize the cracks were beginning to show until Chette came into my office after practice one afternoon. He asked about Sydney and Rosemary; he always asked about them first. Then he asked me how I was holding up.

"I'm okay," I said.

"Eddie," he said, "you can't deal with this in your own strength. You've got a God-size problem."

"What do you mean?"

"I mean you and Rosemary can't handle this on your own. You have to give it to God."

Now, I know that sounds overly simple. The Lord was not a part of my life at that time, and I wasn't so sure about simply saying, "God, you take this problem; we can't handle it." But we were desperate.

For the rest of the afternoon and evening I thought about what Chette was proposing, wondering what God might do. When I got home Rosemary and I knelt with Sydney and prayed, "Lord, this is too big for us. We are going to submit Sydney and her illness to You, and we're going to have faith in You to do Your will in her life and ours."

Almost instantly I experienced a lightness that I would much later understand as the peace described by Christ:

> "Peace I leave with you, my peace I give to you; not as
> the world gives do I give to you. Let not your hearts be
> troubled."
>
> —John 14:27 (NKJV)

From that day forward, amazing things have happened to us. Sydney continued to struggle every day, but we accepted each day God gave us with her as a blessing, and we were very thankful. Instead of living for only a few months, she was with us for almost six years. We experienced so many hard times, we finally stopped asking why. During the long, bad nights we just prayed that she wouldn't suffer anymore.

Lakeba and I prayed with Eddie and Rosemary often. We watched them grow, and we grew with them. Eddie's players also prayed with him and for the Grans, and their prayers were transforming. Travaris Robinson was one of the first players Eddie recruited to Auburn.

"People say things on the field that you would never hear them say out in the world," T-Rob says, "and their excuse is, 'It's football. It's a manly, manly sport.'

"Coach Gran was a man who didn't care what came out of his mouth or what he said to a particular player. Sydney changed all that. She brought us all together. I never would have thought Coach Gran would have become such a man of God, but it's true."

A plaque hangs on the wall of the Grans' home:

> Trust in the LORD with all your heart
> And lean not on your own understanding;
> In all your ways acknowledge him,
> And he will make your paths straight.
> —Proverbs 3:5–6

"Through Sydney, God saved my life," Eddie says. "She gave me eternity. And our two older girls are on fire for Jesus Christ. When I was their age (thirteen and ten), I didn't even know who Jesus was.

"I became a better coach, better husband, and better father. When I didn't have Jesus Christ in my life, I was grasping at all the things the world offered. Now I'm more focused than I have ever been. I don't swear anymore—well, I slip up once in a while, but now I am conscious of it, sorry for it, and know that I am forgiven."

Some mornings God reveals Himself in the beauty of the sunrise. Some days we see His touch in the incredible athletes He has created. And then there are the days when we hear His still, small voice calling to us from the imperfect, the broken, the hurting. We reach out and hold that one close, and He transforms us forever.

21

CALLING ON HIS NAME

"They will call on my name
And I will answer them;
I will say, 'They are my people,'
And they will say, 'The LORD is our God.' "

ZECHARIAH 13:9

The Lord had a message for the Auburn football team: "I want you to pray more. I want you to praise Me and call on My name. And when you do, I will come alongside you." But God didn't just give the message to us. He prepared us for it with a forty-day trial, then He raised up His messenger at just the right time. The result has been a team that prays as powerfully as any church I have been associated with.

The story begins with the messenger. Heath Evans arrived at Auburn two years before I did. As a senior at The King's Academy in West Palm Beach, he had led the state of Florida in scoring his senior year with thirty-two touchdowns and had rushed for almost 2,300 yards. He had grown up in the cocoon of a Christian home (his parents were action-oriented, faith-oriented Christians) and a private Christian high school. Until he came to Auburn, his whole world had been wrapped up in football and Jesus Christ. Once on campus, where he expected his teammates, coaches, and fellow students to be as alive for Christ as he was, he became disillusioned by some who reminded him of Matthew 23:27: "You are like whitewashed tombs, which look beautiful on the outside but on the inside are full of dead men's bones and everything unclean."

I think of the young Moses, who left Pharaoh's palace with his own idea of God's plan for his life. When he saw an Egyptian mistreating an Israelite, he did what he thought God wanted him to do: he killed the Egyptian. Heath didn't kill anybody for the Lord, but like Moses, his righteous indignation led to his own time in the desert. In his time of testing, Heath strayed from the right path. He did what he wanted, and it cost him severely. Recalling his freshman year, he says today, "The consequence of sin is death—not my earthly death, but I felt like it was."

On the football field, though, Heath excelled. He was the starting fullback as a redshirt freshman for Coach Terry Bowden, and he quickly became an impact player. He ran for a touchdown in the second game against Ole Miss, then scored on a fifty-four-yard reception the next week against LSU. A few plays after that great catch and run, though, Heath broke his ankle. By the time he came back for the Georgia game, Bowden was gone as head coach, and Heath's once-promising future appeared in doubt.

I met Heath when I came to Auburn the next summer, 1999, and he had regained his spiritual orientation. Everything I heard about him from other players confirmed my first impression that he was a man of honor and integrity, a Christian who lived out his faith. Now, however, he was about to live a nightmare on the field. He was facing a challenge that would threaten his career—and allow God to use him to transform the team.

Coach Tuberville installed a one-back offense—tailback, not fullback. At Ole Miss a year earlier, his one back had been Deuce McAllister, the best running back in school history, and Heath, the coaches believed, did not fit that mold. "You look at a big, white running back, you're not going to think tailback," Heath told a *Birmingham News* reporter. So he began to sit through his sophomore season with literally no hope of significant playing time. Ever. In the first three games of the season, all wins for Auburn, Heath ran the ball only fourteen times for thirty-one yards. He didn't know it, but God was preparing him.

Then God began to prepare the rest of us for His message. For forty days we experienced a desert dryness. The record will show that Auburn lost five games in a row for the first time since 1952. Now I'm not saying that God made Auburn lose those games any more than I believe God gave Auburn the wins that followed. God didn't cause players to be injured, and He didn't plant ideas in coaches' minds to play one guy and not another. But there are times when God withdraws His blessings to find out if we have been relying on the blessings or on God Himself. That forty-day period, I believe, was one of those times.

DAY ONE, SATURDAY, SEPTEMBER 25: Auburn had won its first three games under Coach Tuberville, including a 41–7 rout of LSU in Baton Rouge in game three. On this day, however, we couldn't beat Ole Miss, the team Tommy had built over the previous four years, the team Auburn had beaten six straight times. To compound our trouble during the 24–17 overtime loss, our starting quarterback, Ben Leard, left the game with a shoulder injury that would keep him on the sidelines for three weeks. Heath Evans didn't carry the ball a single time.

DAY EIGHT, SATURDAY, OCTOBER 2: Auburn got nothing going against seventh-ranked Tennessee, losing 24–0, and it became clear that some SEC teams had a lot more talent on the field than we did. Once again, Heath did not rush with the football a single time, although he caught two passes for twenty-eight yards. At practice nobody worked harder, but when the coaches considered moving Heath to defense, he began to think about transferring to another school.

DAY FOURTEEN, FRIDAY, OCTOBER 8: Previous Auburn football teams had a local pastor who served as chaplain and on Saturday mornings offered a devotional to a few of the players. Coach Tuberville changed all that. He scheduled my devotional for Friday night before games, after the entire team had finished dinner together. He wanted to make sure every player heard the message. That night I focused on our team Scripture, Jeremiah 29:11, and reminded the guys that God was working in us and through us. "He has a plan for each of us and for our team," I said. We just couldn't see that plan yet.

DAY FIFTEEN, SATURDAY, OCTOBER 9: This game may have been the most crushing blow of all. Mississippi State came to Auburn unbeaten and ranked fourteenth in the country. Our defense played its best game of the season, and with three minutes left in the game, we led 16–3. Then in the final two and a half minutes, State scored a touchdown, tackled our punter in the end zone for a safety, then scored another touchdown with nineteen seconds on the clock to win 18–16. I couldn't remember a quieter, more dejected locker room. We had the win right there in our hands and let it slip away. Once again, Heath spent most of the game on the sidelines, running the ball only twice and catching one pass. The coaches put him in on defense for a while, and he tackled Dicenzo Miller after a five-yard run. The season might not have been so frustrating for him if the other running backs had been doing well. They rushed for thirty-nine yards.

DAY TWENTY-TWO, SATURDAY, OCTOBER 16: The desert somehow became drier. Auburn ran the ball twenty-five times against Florida for one yard. That's right. One yard. Heath never touched the ball in a 32–14 loss.

DAY THIRTY-FOUR, FRIDAY, OCTOBER 29: After an off week, when players got over minor injuries, we prepared to play Arkansas. On Friday afternoon we boarded the charter plane for Fayetteville. Heath was carrying a book, *Fresh Wind, Fresh Fire*, by Jim Cymbala, pastor of the Brooklyn Tabernacle. Through Cymbala, God had transformed a broken-down church with fewer than twenty members into a vital six-thousand-member congregation. The plane took off, and Heath started reading what the cover notes described as a "testament of what God can do when men and women begin to pour out their hearts to God." He reached page 19 and realized God was speaking directly to him through this book as the author described his struggle to keep the church doors open:

> That evening, when I was at my lowest, confounded by obstacles, bewildered by the darkness that surrounded us, unable even to continue preaching, I discovered an astonishing truth: God is attracted to weakness. He can't resist those who humbly and honestly admit how desperately they need Him. Our weakness, in fact, makes room for His power.

That's it, Heath thought. *God is attracted to weakness. My weakness. Our weakness.* Heath had always lived his life from a position of strength. At six feet, 235 pounds, he was physically strong and imposing. His parents provided financial stability in the home, and except for his freshman year at Auburn, Heath had experienced spiritual strength as well. But now as he looked at his life, having had the football literally stripped away from him, he saw that he had relied too much on his own strength and not on God. As big and strong as he was, he wasn't strong enough to stand alone. He continued reading until he reached the statement that would transform us:

> If we call upon the Lord, He has promised in His Word to answer, to bring the unsaved to Himself, to pour out His Spirit among us.

That was the promise Heath needed and our entire team needed. In that airplane somewhere high over Mississippi, Heath knew the Lord was calling him to deliver it. But when? And how? His platform was in FCA, where attendance was growing but fewer than half the players attended regularly. Every week they talked about their need to pray more. That's not where God wanted this message delivered. No, God wanted Heath to speak to the entire team. Heath prayed, "Lord, you're going to have to create the opportunity. I can stand up and talk, but somehow you must give me authority so they will listen."

DAY THIRTY-FIVE, SATURDAY, OCTOBER 30: Another miserable game for Auburn. Playing in the rain, Arkansas led 34–3 and Auburn had less than twenty yards rushing midway through the third quarter. Might as well give Heath a shot. Well, Heath Evans took his shot and ran with it, pounding right, left, and up the middle. He ran with fire and confidence that the offensive line caught, and suddenly Auburn was moving up the field. He scored Auburn's first rushing touchdown in five weeks and finished the game with sixty-eight yards rushing, six yards receiving, and a fifteen-yard kickoff return. It was still a 34–10 loss, but at least we saw a glimmer. All the way home Heath played the fourth quarter and that touchdown over in his mind, and between plays he went back to the words he had read the day before. "If we call upon the Lord, He has promised . . ."

DAY FORTY, THURSDAY, NOVEMBER 4: Every Thursday night during the season the team elected the next game's captain, usually based on the previous game's performance. On this night they elected Heath Evans to be offensive captain. This was the platform Heath had prayed for. He realized that now was the time to deliver the message. He had brought *Fresh Wind, Fresh Fire* with him, and he held it when he stood to speak.

"Hey, guys," he said, "you know it's been a trying year for me—a tough year for all of us—and the Lord has placed a lot on my heart. I've been reading this book and thinking about some principles. One thing is prayer. I believe if we will pray together, we will stay together, no matter how tough things get. God promises that when we pray, He is bound by His name to come to us. So I'd like to have a prayer meeting Friday night after our team meetings, and whoever wants to come can come. We won't be praying about football. That will be the least of our concerns. Instead, we'll pray about our family and things outside of football."

As Heath spoke, something like a breath of fresh air blew through the room. The Holy Spirit was moving among us. On Friday night, day one of our life together on the other side of the desert, together we would call on the Lord.

22

FROM THE MOUNTAINTOP OF PRAYER TO THE VALLEY OF TEMPTATION

Jesus . . . led them up a high mountain by themselves.

MATTHEW 17:1

Heath Evans couldn't have imagined how many lives would be changed when he followed the Lord's prompting and led us to pray as a team on that Friday night in 1999. After dinner and our devotional, the offensive and defensive coordinators spent an hour with their players going over final instructions. Then, as everybody spilled out into the hallway, Heath stood by the door into the room where the offensive players had met, and by his presence alone he reminded his teammates that we would be gathering together to pray. Twenty-five or so players and coaches came into the room. We pulled chairs into a circle and dimmed the lights, and Heath read a few verses of Scripture. Then he told us what was on his heart before asking if there were any prayer requests.

He had worked out the procedure on his own, and when the first request was stated, he asked another player to pray. We closed our eyes, held hands, and the player lifted the individual request. With his *amen*, the room fell silent until another player or coach made a request or offered a praise. Lifting up one concern or praise at a time allowed us to fully concentrate on that player's prayer. With each prayer I could feel burdens being lifted as we literally cast our cares on the Lord. In stating our prayer requests aloud, we were also fulfilling Galatians 6:2: "Carry each other's burdens, and in this way you will fulfill the law of Christ." We felt compassion for one another, and in our compassion, which means "to suffer with," we were being changed. Coaches and players spoke in ways they never had on the field or in meetings. A position coach told the team about his daughter's severe illness. A player said his parents were struggling to hold their marriage together. Another player's little brother had become caught up in drugs. We prayed for each of them. An injured player feared he might never again enjoy the love of the game; that was as close as we got to actually praying for football. Many of us shed tears. After nearly an hour of prayers, the room remained silent, and Heath asked me to close with a final prayer. With that we stood and looked at each other as new creations, having seen teammates' and coaches' hearts for the first time. I sensed a glow from each face. Christ had taken us to the mountaintop.

A week later, at our second prayer meeting, attendance doubled, and on the night before the Alabama game, all but two players prayed together. In three Friday nights we had solidified a tradition of prayer that binds Auburn football players past, present, and future. Then we stepped out of the prayer room back into the world.

As much as we might have wanted to live in the ecstasy of our encounters with Christ in the prayer room, He called us down from the mountaintop to live in the valley, where we faced drudgery, temptation, and demons. Wayne Hall had reminded me about the valley several months earlier. Wayne had been one of my coaches in the 1980s and has since undergone one of the most dramatic spiritual transformations I have ever seen. He truly loves the Lord and is now a close prayer partner. The first week I arrived back at Auburn, Wayne took me aside and told me, "Chette, you'd better be ready. You're going into a dark world."

Wayne understood the ongoing spiritual warfare in the world of Division I college football. He understood the stronghold the enemy has in that world—the lust of the flesh, lust of the eyes, and pride of life that the Bible warns us about (1 John 2:16). College football is wrapped up in these things. Players walk down the street, and girls, total strangers, introduce themselves and give them their phone numbers. Every Saturday night they're invited to parties all over town. And on Saturday afternoon they run into that huge valley surrounded on all sides by a mountain of adoring fans who place them on a pedestal, and they can easily be consumed by pride.

The good news of the valley lies in Mark 9:9: As Jesus' disciples were coming down from the mountain, Jesus came with them. He didn't send them into the valley alone. And He accompanies us into every valley. We know that. In the valley the disciples encountered a demon, and Jesus told them that it could be removed only through prayer. So we pray—on the mountaintop and in the valley, where we find ourselves almost every day.

Late one afternoon in 2006 Robert Dunn ran off the practice field after returning a punt and stood beside me. Another player ran over and said to Robert, "Hey, I need to holler at you, man."

"What is it?" Robert asked.

The other player realized I was standing there and said, "Aw, no, man, Brother Chette's right there." (That happens a lot. Guys see "Brother Chette" and they duck down or turn the other way.)

"Go ahead and tell me," Robert said.

"It's a girl, man. One of my girls wants to holler at you."

"Man, get away from me with that," Robert said. "I'm trying to focus."

I spoke up then and said, "Yeah, you got to focus for the game."

"Naw, it's not the game, Brother Chette," Robert said. "Focus on life. Focus on life, not just the game."

Robert had met the Master on the mountaintop, and now he was calling on His strength in the valley. The next morning I remembered what Robert said as I led the coaches through their weekly devotional. The Scripture was Philippians 3:14: "I press toward the goal for the prize of the upward call of God in Jesus Christ" (NKJV).

An FCA Bible devotional told the story of an Olympic athlete who was running in the final heat for a place on the Olympic team. Unsure where the finish line was, she asked and was told that the finish line would be at the starting line. The starter's gun fired and she raced ahead of the pack around the track, crossing the starting line first. Then dismayed, she w atched as the other runners raced past her. The finish line was actually a few yards ahead of the starting line.

Our players set goals for their lives, and many of them fall short because the demons in the valley distract them from the true finish line. Robert Dunn knew he had to maintain his focus on his finish line and not let anybody turn him from it.

Focus begins and ends in prayer. Through the years the media have written and spoken of our team's prayers in the end zone and on the sidelines. They wrote about Courtney Taylor kneeling in prayer instead of jumping in jubilation when he caught the touchdown pass that beat LSU 10–9 in 2004. Later the same year, television announcers talked about our guys praying on the field after Junior Rosegreen collided with Georgia's Reggie Brown, knocking Brown out cold. Our guys—the entire team—took off their helmets and knelt in prayer, and for five minutes the stadium remained quiet as fans joined them.

People were watching. I never realized the public impact of the players' private moments of prayer on the field until a freshman running back stood up in front of the team in the prayer room in 2006 and said, "You were my heroes when I was in high school. I watched y'all every week, and my teammates and I imitated you on the field with hookups going onto the field and praying after you scored a touchdown."

He had seen the public response to a private and powerful time of prayer that began when one player said, "This is what we have to do."

> "They will call on my name
> And I will answer them;
> I will say, 'They are my people,'
> And they will say, 'The LORD is our God.' "
> —Zechariah 13:9

23

HE WILL NOT FORGET

"I will not forget you!
See, I have engraved you on the palms of my hands."
Isaiah 49:15–16

Every day Rashaud Walker looks at the name *Gwen* on his forearm and remembers his mother. Gwen Walker radiated joy. Whenever she came to Auburn to visit Rashaud, she cooked—sometimes barbecue, sometimes catfish, always delicious—and Rashaud's apartment would suddenly fill with his teammates sharing the bounty. It was always a time of laughter when Gwen was around. She wasn't just a football mom, she was a team mom, and I never saw her without a smile.

Most weeks Gwen and Rashaud talked on the telephone almost every day. Rashaud didn't care if some of the guys thought he was a momma's boy; Gwen was his best friend. His father, William Baker, said, "Sometimes, they're more like brother and sister than son and mom." In the lead-up to the Florida game in 2001, they had plenty to talk about. Florida had beaten Auburn twice the year before, in the regular season and the SEC Championship, by a combined total of 66–13. Rashaud, defensive back and the fifth-leading tackler on the team that year, had made only two solo tackles and one assist in the two games as Florida quarterback Rex Grossman threw for nine touchdowns.

Now Florida was coming to Auburn ranked No. 1 in the nation, and Grossman was having another spectacular year. At 4–1, Auburn was unranked and a twenty-one-point underdog. Rashaud's roommate, linebacker Tavarreus Pounds, had sprained his ankle a week earlier against Mississippi State and couldn't play, adding to the defensive load.

At a few minutes before 5 o'clock on Saturday afternoon, Rashaud's parents stood in the crowd wearing their Auburn jerseys with Rashaud's number, 37, waiting for Tiger Walk—when the players walk from the athletic dorm down to the stadium through thousands of cheering fans. Rashaud walked with his teammates through the sea of blue and orange, and Gwen wanted to hug him. He would have hugged her back right there, but they both just said, "I love you." Then Gwen and William went to their seats in the stadium.

Most of the players were in their uniforms, and some were stretching when I came into the locker room an hour later. They all have their own final pregame routines. Some listen to music, others talk quietly with teammates and review last-minute instructions from coaches, a few seem to be staring into their lockers. I stood beside a drink box watching and praying silently for these young men. Rashaud came over and asked, "Pray for me, Brother Chette?" We knelt there and held right hands and I prayed, "God, I thank You for the relationship I have with Rashaud, but even more, I thank You for the relationship Rashaud has with You. You have blessed Rashaud with gifts and talents. Today we pray that You would allow Rashaud to use those gifts and talents to go out there and help this team, but more importantly, to give You praise and glory and to be the leader out there that his teammates need to see. Amen." Then Reggie Torbor came over, Jason Campbell, Carnell Williams, and a dozen more, and I prayed a similar prayer for each of them.

Finally Coach Tuberville called the team to the center of the room, told them what it would mean to beat the top-ranked team in the country, then asked me to pray. When I said, "Amen," he said, "All right, let's go get 'em." The players and coaches ran out from the locker room, with the stadium rocking above us and the ground shaking below us from all the cheering and stomping. I couldn't remember ever hearing it that loud. I stepped through the tunnel onto the field, and my ears were instantly ringing from the noise.

I looked into the stands and spotted Lakeba and our children, and I saw some of the players looking up too. At some point before every game they all find their families in the stands. Rashaud spotted Gwen and William wearing their 37s, waving and smiling.

Then I found my place on the sidelines for the kickoff, right at sunset. On Florida's first play from scrimmage, Rex Grossman threw a sideline pass that Rashaud broke up, and somehow the cheering grew even louder. That's the way it would go all night as Rashaud played the flats like he owned them, breaking up passes and making tackles for losses or short gains. With ten seconds left in the game, Damon Duval kicked a field goal into the night to upset Florida 23–20. We ran to midfield to pray with players from Florida as fans poured out of the stands and started pulling down the south end-zone goalpost.

Rashaud was still living in the glow on Monday morning when Gwen called to tell him she had just heard the news that he had been named SEC Defensive Player of the Week. Like always, Rashaud and Gwen talked several more times in the week leading up to the Louisiana Tech game, which Auburn won much less enthusiastically, 48–41. On the following Monday morning Rashaud's phone rang again while he was getting ready for class. It was not Gwen, but a police detective from back home in Georgia, telling him to go to Coach Tuberville's office. He wouldn't say why, but Rashaud knew it couldn't be good. He decided to put off the bad news and go to class.

A few minutes after 8 a.m., Coach Tuberville came into my office and told me that Gwen Walker had been killed in a traffic accident. Driving to work at Stone Mountain Middle School, the car ahead of her had crossed a railroad track and stopped, then Gwen pulled up behind it, stopping on the track. Another car pulled up close behind. Moments later Gwen must have seen the train coming, but had nowhere to go with the car and was not able to get out and run before the train hit and killed her.

Tommy asked me to go get Rashaud from class. I walked out to my car praying with every step, "Lord, please tell me what to say to this boy." Never in seminary had they taught me how to tell a college kid that his mother had been killed. I parked outside Haley Center and walked up to Rashaud's classroom. I told the professor there was an emergency, and Rashaud stepped out into the hall.

"What is it, Brother Chette?" he asked, but I couldn't tell him there. We drove the longest two-minute drive ever back to the Athletic Complex and walked inside, with me continuing to pray all the way. I closed the door, and somehow in that moment I felt a weight lifting off my shoulders. The fear left and I felt peace, as if I didn't have to figure out anything. Quietly the spirit of God was saying, "Just tell the truth."

"Rashaud," I said, "I have some very bad news."

That was six years ago, and I honestly don't remember the words I spoke after the first sentence. I was no longer in control of the moment. The Holy Spirit had taken charge, as Rashaud's words attest:

I still get chills talking about that day. And every time I remember that day and talk about it, I get stronger. In that moment I witnessed the power of God.

When Chette told me about my mom, I was crying like I couldn't stop. Chette held my hand and prayed for a long time, then he read from the Bible: "And God shall wipe away all tears from their eyes; and there shall be no more death, neither sorrow, nor crying, neither shall there be any more pain: for the former things are passed away" (Revelation 21:4 NKJV). As he prayed and read, he was explaining to me the afterlife, how my mom can't get sick and can't be harmed anymore, how because of her relationship with God she was in heaven, and because of my relationship with God I would be with her in heaven someday too. In that moment there was some power, some spirit in the room, and I literally felt my tears rolling back up in my eyes. It was like I was experiencing everything Chette had been teaching us and telling us all those years.

After a while coaches came in one by one to offer their condolences, then players came in. Soon, however, they were back on the practice field preparing for Arkansas, and Rashaud wanted to play. Saturday would be his twenty-second birthday, and his mother wanted him to be on the field.

Rashaud left a ticket at the will-call window for Gwen. His father later told a newspaper reporter, "The first week he played after the accident, I thought he was looking in the stands for her. His mom not being at those games is tough for him. Tough for everybody." Just like against Florida, Rashaud made the first tackle from scrimmage, but after that the game didn't resemble the Florida game at all, as Arkansas won 41–17. Then on Monday morning, a week after the accident, most of the team climbed onto a bus for Atlanta, where we helped Rashaud bury his mother. Tavarreus Pounds and five other teammates served as pallbearers. Soon afterward Rashaud had his mother's name tattooed on his forearm so he would see it and think of her every day.

When the season ended, Rashaud knew he wasn't ready to leave his Auburn family, but he had to work hard in the classroom to earn a spot on the roster in 2002. As an academic partial qualifier in 1998, he had sat out his freshman year and could earn a final year of eligibility only by graduating before the 2002 season began. "I think God made it possible for me to graduate and get that love and those prayers that people were praying for me," he recalls. Then he looks at his forearm again. "That year without Mom was a year of maturing for me. I know there is nothing I can't overcome now. If it doesn't kill me, it will just make me stronger. And when my friends have loved ones who pass or go through hard times, I tell them my testimony. I tell them about that day that I will always remember and what the Spirit did for me."

24

DON'T COME HOME EMPTY-HANDED

"Come, follow me," Jesus said, "and I will make you fishers of men."
MATTHEW 4:19

"Chette, it's Pop," my brother Percy said. You're never ready for that phone call and that tone of voice. I put my hand on the kitchen counter and waited. "He passed out in church. We're at the hospital."

"How is he?" I asked.

"He's awake now. He says he's okay. We're waiting for the doctor."

"Let me talk to him."

Lakeba, the kids, and I were about to walk out the door to church, after the Sunday morning marathon of getting ourselves and three children fed and dressed in our Sunday clothes. Lakeba was back with Chette Jr., who was two years old.

"Hello?" Pop's voice sounded strong, almost normal.

"What's up, Pop?" I asked.

"I'm all right, Son," he said. "Just some heartburn."

"You sure?"

"Sure, I'm sure."

"Well, you make 'em check you out good."

"I'm all right," he insisted.

"Okay, Pop. I love you."

"What is it?" Lakeba asked. She was standing at the kitchen door.

"Pop. He's in the hospital. Passed out in church."

"Is he all right?"

"He sounds pretty good."

Lakeba wasn't convinced and neither was I. Twenty minutes later I was sitting in our church next to her, not hearing what the preacher was saying or what the choir was singing. I was just praying for Pop. My cell phone vibrated in my pocket, and I pulled it out and saw Calvin Jr.'s number. Leaning low, I held it to my ear. "Hello."

"Chette, you better get up here."

"I'm on my way."

I looked at Lakeba, and she nodded, then I stepped out into the aisle and hurried to the door. As soon as I stepped outside, I called Calvin Jr. back. Pop had taken a turn and was unconscious. The doctors were working on him. I ran to the car and scratched off into the street.

"Hold on, Pop, hold on," I said as I sped up I-85. "God, be with him. Please give him strength."

Give him strength. What an odd thing to pray for Pop. He was the strongest man I had ever known. Since I was a kid he had told us about working in the fields when he was a boy and running off to the military as soon as he was old enough. He came back home and refused to return to the farm. Instead, he drove a truck—a decent job, but one that exposed him to his greatest weakness while on the road: women. My father even had a nickname, which I will not repeat here, but that identified his weakness to all who knew him.

We all have weaknesses. We all sin. I do. You do. However, unlike you and me, whose sins are, for the most part, hidden, my father could not escape the public scrutiny of his sin. He became the embodiment of Ephesians 5:12–13, 15:

> It is shameful even to mention what the disobedient do in secret. But everything exposed by the light becomes visible. . . . Be very careful, then, how you live.

Later in his life Pop accepted Christ, and every Sunday he sat on the front row of the church, just as he had previously. Now, however, he took that spot in humility, as "chief among sinners," quoting the apostle Paul. And from my perspective, Pop's humility made him stronger than ever.

I turned hard into the hospital parking lot, parked near the emergency room entrance, and ran inside. My brothers and Lula Mae, Pop's wife, were standing out in the hall looking at the floor. I was too late.

Birth order doesn't matter when there's a death in the family. The minister becomes the leader for a time, even if he's brother number six. They led me down to the room where Pop was—not a room with machines and equipment to keep people alive, but a stark, gray place for the dead, my father, a six-foot-three, 270-pound earthly shell. My brothers and I held hands with my father's wife, and I prayed for him, thanking God for Pop's life and asking Him to receive our father into eternal life.

We scheduled the funeral for Saturday, the same day Auburn would be playing at Ole Miss. I would deliver the message. All week I was on the road from Auburn to Winston and back again, and I used the driving time to formulate my thoughts. I saw Pop coming from a hunting trip loaded down with almost more rabbits than he could carry. Pop never came home from hunting empty-handed. He was the best shot in Winston, and we ate everything he brought home—rabbit, squirrel, whatever. Mama spent all afternoon skinning and cleaning those rabbits, and the next morning she'd cook rabbit gravy and biscuits. Pop never took me hunting, but he took my brothers and me fishing more times than I can remember. All eight of us lined up on the creek bank with cane poles, lines, and hooks with worms or beef liver for bait. We'd fish all day long sitting on buckets, drinking Cokes, and eating peanuts or headcheese Mama had made. Again, we never came home empty-handed. We'd bring a stringer loaded with little bream or big, fat catfish for Mama to fry.

All those memories were wrapped up in Pop as I stepped into the pulpit on Saturday afternoon and looked out at all the people jammed into that little church. Then I opened the Bible and read John 14:9:

"Anyone who has seen me has seen the Father."

My father had given me his strength and his determination, and Christ had given me strength to overcome certain fleshly desires that Pop had succumbed to.

More important than that, I said as I looked down at three women in black dabbing their eyes, Christ had forgiven Pop once and for all the moment he invited Him into his heart. The same Christ had forgiven me, and He was standing at the door knocking, ready to forgive any and all who asked, no matter what.

"I know it's not traditional to offer an invitation to Christ at a funeral," I said, "but I believe it's what Pop would want right now. So I'm asking you, if you're ready to receive the One who saved my father, the One who is right now receiving Pop with open arms, won't you step up?" We sang "Amazing Grace," and I watched six people—several cousins and a couple of others—slide out of their pews and walk up the aisle to meet me at the altar. They all told the congregation that they wanted to receive Christ or recommit their lives to the Lord, and a sad day became a beautiful moment in the Kingdom. Then we carried Pop's casket out from the church, across the road, and up a little hill, where we laid it in the ground under the pine trees. Then we stood in the sunshine sensing lightness that overwhelmed our sorrow. Pop was going home, but he wasn't going empty-handed.

25

A HANDFUL OF MUSTARD SEEDS

"I tell you the truth, if you have faith as small as a mustard seed, you can say to this mountain, 'Move from here to there' and it will move. Nothing will be impossible for you."

MATTHEW 17:20

The Lord tests our faith, not for His sake but for ours, and through our trials we witness the Lord's faithfulness. For Joshua the test came at the walls of Jericho. For David, standing before Goliath. For the disciples, in the storm at sea. Our test came during the 2003 football season.

We had ended the 2002 season with wins over Alabama and then Penn State in the Capital One Bowl. Optimism ran high. Preseason rankings by the *Sporting News* and *The New York Times* in August 2003 put us at No. 1 in the nation.

Then we opened the season with a loss to Southern California, and a week later we lost to Georgia Tech. We rolled down the highway, leaving behind the Atlanta lights and the broken promise of our breakout season, and by the middle of the next week the rumors already swirled. Apparently university president William Walker had lit into athletic director David Housel at Tech's Grant Field, demanding that something be done, or else he would fire Tuberville immediately.

We won five straight games in the coming weeks, including two against top-ten opponents, and calmed the brewing storm temporarily. Then losses to LSU, Ole Miss, and Georgia fueled November discontent. Everybody heard the rumors. Even the coaches' children heard rumors from their elementary school friends. Tommy Tuberville was out. He would be fired by Thanksgiving.

A cyclone of dissension swirled about us, and we felt completely alone. Some of our ministry's strongest supporters were rumored to be leading the charge to have the coaches fired. These were men the coaches had come to trust without reservation, and their apparent betrayal wounded them deeply. The media said the coaches had blown it, and some of our own fans at the LSU and Ole Miss games booed.

Although I never stopped believing God's promise, "Never will I leave you; never will I forsake you" (Hebrews 13:5), there were many days and nights when I prayed that God would reveal Himself more clearly.

In my devotionals during the coaches' weekly staff meetings, we focused on the story of Jesus calming the storm (Mark 4:35-40):

> That day when evening came, he said to his disciples, "Let us go over to the other side." Leaving the crowd behind, they took him along, just as he was, in the boat. There were also other boats with him. A furious squall came up, and the waves broke over the boat, so that it was nearly swamped. Jesus was in the stern, sleeping

on a cushion. The disciples woke him and said to him, "Teacher, don't you care if we drown?"

He got up, rebuked the wind and said to the waves, "Quiet! Be still!" Then the wind died down, and it was completely calm.

The storm became a crisis of faith for the disciples, even though Jesus had told them, "Let us go over to the other side." They should have been confident, just as our coaches and I should have been confident, that if Christ said we were going to the other side of the lake, we were going to make it safely, no matter how big the waves, how hard the wind, or how violent the storm.

For four years Christ had been with us. We had experienced His presence too many times to stop believing. Now, however, He seemed to be withdrawing His tangible blessings from us to teach us to walk by faith in Him even when we were not feeling His presence in every moment.

"God doesn't want us to panic in this situation," I told the coaches week after week. "He has everything under control." We prayed together and believed His promise that He was with us. Then we would walk out of the meeting room confident that we were in God's will, until the phone rang, we heard another rumor, and we jumped right back into the fears of our flesh.

Tommy was the only one among us who remained calm, even upbeat, throughout the season. He came into my office more in 2003 than in any year before or since, and I spent more time in his office as well. I was supposed to be the team chaplain, but for the last half of that season, he and Lakeba were my spiritual leaders.

Yet even Tommy grew frustrated at times. With God's help he had built a foundation on something more solid than wins alone. He was fulfilling his promise to our players' parents to help their sons grow as responsible young men. "Now after all the hard work we've done," he said, "we have four or five people who don't believe in us. And whether we can get it done or not, they don't have the patience and persistence. They don't believe we can get it done."

We came into the week of the Alabama game with a 6–5 record. By then the decision had been made. Win or lose, Tommy and his staff would be replaced. Somehow, Tommy remained at peace throughout the week. "I never believed we would be gone," he said later. "God kept giving me faith. I slept well every night."

I was reminded of Job's declaration: "Though he slay me, yet will I trust in him" (Job 13:15 KJV).

While Tommy was experiencing peace that he could not explain except by faith, behind the scenes, one of the most embarrassing events in the life of Auburn athletics was unfolding. Two days before the Alabama game, the university president, athletic director, and two trustees flew up to interview Louisville head coach Bobby Petrino—without asking permission from Louisville officials or telling Tommy that his job was in jeopardy.

On Saturday Auburn beat Alabama 28–23, and by Monday the clandestine interview had been discovered and was made public in the media.

"When it was all told what was happening behind the scenes," Tommy said later, "I believe God was saying, 'Listen, it's not over. You're going to be given a stage where you can do more.'"

He believed the truth told through Joseph, who was sold into slavery by his brothers and later told them, "You intended to harm me, but God intended it for good to accomplish what is now being done" (Genesis 50:20). He also believed Romans 8:28: "And we know that in all things God works for the good of those who love him, who have been called according to his purpose."

No matter how bad things seemed to us, Tommy believed God would take those circumstances and create something good.

26

SURRENDER AND TRUST

"I will give your life to you as a prize in all places, wherever you go."
Jeremiah 45:5 (NKJV)

"The biggest thing about life is God gave His life for us," Coach Tuberville says, "and the toughest thing about life for us is to surrender our life and follow Him. That's what He's asking us to do. He's asking us, players and coaches, to surrender a lot of things."

He's asking us to surrender *everything*! And He makes no promise of earthly reward in return: no promise of an undefeated season, no promise of a bowl game, not even the promise of a single win. Instead, he promises something infinitely greater—your life. Life so fresh and new you don't even recognize it.

In a similar way, a football coach asks his players to sacrifice themselves to a larger purpose. Tom Landry, the great Dallas Cowboys coach, summed it up this way: the coach must lead men "to do what they don't want to do so they can become what they want to become." Notice he didn't say, "to get," but "to become."

Become what? Alive!

Defensive tackle Wayne Dickens looks back on the 2003 season and recalls, "We lost five games, and everybody was looking around asking why. Nobody had any answers, but I think it was because so many guys were trying to do it their own way."

At the last team meeting before off-season workouts started, he remembers Coach Tuberville's simple message that the players had better be prepared to surrender to the team: "I know y'all probably heard about everything that happened. They tried to get rid of me. Some of y'all probably wanted me gone too, but I'm here. So now you can choose to be with us, or you can hit the door."

The words look harsh on paper, but Tommy knew the foundation for building winners required 100 percent commitment from each player. He told them that the next eight months before the 2004 season began would be as demanding as any they had ever experienced, then he asked the same question Jesus asked: "Do you also want to go away?" (John 6:67).

Every man stayed, including Carnell Williams, Ronnie Brown, and Carlos Rogers, who had considered passing up their senior season for the NFL. Then two coaches gave their players a living example of surrender. Hugh Nall and Steve Ensminger, who had been offensive coordinator and quarterbacks coach in 2003, agreed to take lower-profile positions so Tommy could bring in a new man as offensive coordinator. Neither Hugh nor Steve had a choice about keeping his former job, but lesser men might have stormed away or stayed and sowed seeds of bitterness. Instead, they became part of the hiring process that brought Al Borges to Auburn, and the three men worked closely together, along with Greg Knox and Eddie Gran, to build a championship-caliber offense.

Trust. I couldn't get the word out of my mind. Before surrendering one must trust. We had lost a lot of trust in 2003, and not just because of the behind-the-scenes manipulations. We lost five games on the field, not in administrators' offices. Going forward, players had to trust coaches and each other. Coaches had to trust players and their fellow coaches.

More than ever before, in 2004 we learned to trust God for everything. Jesus tells us, "Do not worry about your life, what you will eat or drink; or about your body, what you will wear" (Matthew 6:25). He had our jobs and our lives in His hands. For five years our team Scripture had been Jeremiah 29:11, and we continued to believe God's promise. After all that had happened in 2003, though, the Lord led us to a new Scripture for 2004:

> Trust in the LORD with all your heart
> And lean not on your own understanding;
> In all your ways acknowledge him,
> And he will make your paths straight.
> —Proverbs 3:5–6

Trust God and trust each other. It was a simple message. Through the summer, players and I met for weekly Bible study and hot wings. I met with several of the coaches for Bible study and saw all of them almost every day in the hallway of the Athletic Complex or in their offices. As we drew closer to the Lord, He convicted several coaches regarding their cussing. Foul language is an unfortunate way of life for many coaches at the college level, and we had a couple of coaches who were masters at it. When they told me they were going to try to stop cussing, the hair on my arms literally stood on end. What a witness it would be if they could make good on that commitment! Players seeing that would know the Holy Spirit was in our midst.

On the night before our first game against Louisiana-Monroe, I gave the players T-shirts with TRUST and the team Scripture printed on the back. On Saturday morning at Tiger Walk, many of the players were wearing their T-shirts. Players looking at teammates walking in front of them got the message: *Trust God and trust me.*

Jason Campbell had a good, not great, start at quarterback against Louisiana-Monroe. After one quarter we led 10–0. To start the second quarter the coaches sent in redshirt freshman Brandon Cox, who led a seventy-one-yard scoring drive that included a thirty-nine-yard completion to Courtney Taylor. Brandon ran fourteen yards for the touchdown. It's unusual, but not unheard of, for the backup quarterback to play in the first half of the opening game. Brandon had earned his opportunity with a great spring and a strong preseason. Jason went back onto the field the next series, and after driving sixty yards he threw an interception. Then he went right back in on the next drive, and I heard some people in the stands booing him. They wanted the new kid. That drive stalled and we punted right before halftime. As the team ran off the field, I heard more boos.

Trust. It didn't extend to some fans in the stands. They trusted Carnell and Ronnie, but they didn't trust Jason. In practice the next week, Brandon worked several series with the first-team offense. Jason stood on the sidelines, and I had never seen him so angry. "I'm not putting up with this again this season," he said. "This is my senior year, and it ain't gonna happen." In four years since his redshirt year, Jason had been led by four different offensive coordinators. For two years he had shared the starting job with Daniel Cobb, and he wasn't willing to go back to that arrangement with anybody. I don't know if the coaches were trying to pump him up by playing Brandon, but Jason left the field that day wondering if they trusted him to run Coach Borges's new offense. He and I met and talked for a long time, and we continued to get together whenever we could and work through stuff and pray.

In my years at Auburn I've seen God make dramatic changes in the lives of many players. And I've seen others, like Jason, arrive on campus already committed to the Lord and needing a mentor more than an evangelist. Some people look at Jason's success in 2004 (he was named SEC Player of the Year) and wonder what changed from previous years. Jason didn't transform overnight. Physically, he used his skills to take advantage of the talent around him to succeed. Mentally and spiritually, he grew through the adversity he experienced, and he learned to trust. Through those prayers, Jason learned to surrender, put his faith in God, and worry less. In return, God gave Jason's life to him as a prize.

27

LEARNING TO FORGIVE

Get rid of all bitterness, rage and anger, brawling and slander,
along with every form of malice. Be kind and compassionate to one
another, forgiving each other, just as in Christ God forgave you.

EPHESIANS 4:31–32

Early every morning Tommy Jackson walked through the athletic building just to say hello to the coaches on his way to his workout. T.J., a 300-pound noseguard, was always talking, always smiling, no matter what. "When I was young," T.J. says, "my mother told me to love people, and I always have. The Lord put that love in me, and my mother brought it out.

"Sometimes, though, I smile when I'm hurting on the inside, and I hope the hurt will go away."

The summer of 2004 was one of those hurting times. Like too many young African Americans, T.J. had grown up in a single-parent home. Now at age twenty, he was filled with two decades' worth of resentment for his earthly father that ran counter to the love his heavenly Father had put in his heart, and he didn't know what to do with it.

"You've got to let go of all that bitterness," I told him. "There's no way you can be an effective Christian with all that hatred in your heart for your dad. You need to go see your father and forgive him."

I knew from experience that this was the only way. In the weeks following my own salvation twenty years earlier, I had continued to carry bitterness, even hatred, for my father because of his unfaithfulness to my mom. Kyle Collins, who had led me to Christ, told me almost the exact same words I told T.J.: "You have to reconcile with your father. You have to forgive him." Then Kyle shared with me Matthew 5:23–24:

> "Therefore, if you are offering your gift at the altar and there remember that your brother has something against you, leave your gift there in front of the altar. First go and be reconciled to your brother; then come and offer your gift."

It's ironic that the hardest people to talk to about conversion and forgiveness are the people who love you most. I would have given almost anything to avoid talking to my father about it. Every day I thought about it and put it off until I finally drove home and sat with him. We talked, and I asked him to forgive me for the trouble I had caused and for the bitter feeling I had held for him. Then I told him I forgave him. As I did, I could feel a physical weight lifted from me, and over time we were able to build a spirit of unity that transcended our father/son relationship.

I knew the weight T.J. was carrying around would continue to burden him until he put it aside.

A few days later T.J. called his father and arranged to meet him at his grandmother's house. He drove to Opelika with the same sweaty palms and the same nervous stomach I had experienced. It was not going to be easy for T.J. to say, "I forgive you," to a man who didn't believe he needed forgiveness. They sat on the front porch and talked while T.J.'s grandmother stayed inside and a bunch of nephews and cousins played around the house. Neither T.J. nor his dad was exactly sure what to say. As they searched for the words that might heal the wounds in their relationship, an argument broke out somewhere way down the street. A gun was fired, and T.J.'s father somehow instinctively jumped in front of his son and was hit by a bullet. T.J. caught his father in his arms and held him until an ambulance arrived, then rode with him to the hospital. The bullet had penetrated Thomas Jackson Sr.'s stomach and liver, but he survived.

While his father recovered in the hospital with T.J. at his side, the two grew closer. But after he was released, the father's issues and addictions came between them again. T.J. wishes the experience could have brought his father and him into a stronger, mutually loving relationship.

"But that's not what it was about," T.J. says. "It wasn't about me or my dad or Chette Williams. It was about God. It was an awakening for me, and it helped me understand why God has us here."

Having his father risk his life to save him, T.J. came to understand Jesus' words:

> "Which of you fathers, if your son asks for a fish, will give him a snake instead? Or if he asks for an egg, will give him a scorpion? If you then, though you are evil, know how to give good gifts to your children, how much more will your Father in heaven give the Holy Spirit to those who ask him!"
> —Luke 11:11–13

What did God have in store for T.J.? For weeks he told almost no one about the shooting or about the promising, then disappointing, relationship with his father. "I was going to deal with it the way I do," he says, "still smiling and hurting on the inside and hoping it would go away."

At that point I thought he needed the support of his teammates, and they couldn't help him if he didn't tell them what he was going through. So I encouraged him to share it with the team.

On a September Friday night in the prayer room, T.J. stood up and told his story. He told us about his childhood and the root of his anger with his father. He took us in our minds to his grandmother's front porch, the sound of the shot, his slumping father, and the wail of the ambulance. He told us about sitting at his father's bedside in the hospital and the hope of a budding friendship, and then of the disappointment as his father slid back into his former ways. And through it all, T.J. said his faith in God grew.

"God never wants me to worry," he said. "God asks us to 'put your faith in Me. Love Me. Let Me be God and I will do what needs to be done.' God is taking care of me."

In the dark room I heard tears being sniffed back from several directions, some for T.J. and, I'm sure, some for themselves and their own fathers. We prayed for T.J. and his father, and for once I looked forward to the end of our prayers, when we would all put our arms around our brother. I had encouraged him to tell his story so his teammates could support him; instead, the Holy Spirit used this experience to unify us and strengthen us individually and as a team.

28

HARD FIGHTING SOLDIERS

*"You will receive power when the Holy Spirit comes on you; and you
will be my witnesses in Jerusalem, and in all Judea and Samaria,
and to the ends of the earth."*

ACTS 1:8

We thought we knew what it meant to trust. Then God showed us a
whole new way.

The week of the Tennessee game in 2004, we sat 4–0. Tennessee
was ranked tenth in the nation, we were eighth, and we would be playing in Neyland Stadium, Knoxville, in front of more than 107,000
screaming fans and on ESPN, which would be telecasting GameDay
from Knoxville.

On Monday morning I started planning my Friday night devotional. I pulled a gold medallion from my desk drawer and looked at
the Roman soldier on the back. The soldier's armor had a hook that he
used to attach himself to the soldier beside him, and when they faced
an enemy, the soldiers knew they were fighting for themselves and for

the men they were hooked to. Because if that guy got wounded, you had to carry him through. That, I believed, would be a strong image of trust, and a reminder that we must also be trustworthy.

On Wednesday night we gathered in the basement of the Athletic Complex for pizza and our weekly FCA meeting, and when the time came for the meeting to start, the guy I had asked to lead the music hadn't shown up. Kyle Derozan, a sophomore tight end from a tiny town in Louisiana, had sung a few times during our summertime Bible study, so I pulled him aside and asked him to lead us.

He agreed, and after I opened the meeting with a prayer, Kyle stood and said, "I'm gonna sing y'all this song I knew growing up. It's called 'Hard Fighting Soldier.'"

He started singing, and I was struck by the timing of the battle imagery—just as I was planning a devotional on the same theme.

> I am a hard fighting soldier, on the battlefield.
> I am a hard fighting soldier, on the battlefield.
> I am a hard fighting soldier, on the battlefield.
> I keep on bringing souls to Jesus
> By the service that I give.*

On Friday night in the Knoxville hotel banquet room, I brought out the medallion and reminded the team of our commitment to trust in the Lord and each other. I told them about the Roman soldiers hooking together going into battle. "That's what you've got to do," I said. "You have to hook up with your teammate and protect him while you fight side by side."

An hour later we came back together in the prayer room and turned down the lights. As we neared the end of our prayer time, Stanley

* Copyright © Cecil O. Lyde

McGlover asked Kyle to sing "Hard Fighting Soldier" for us. He did, only this time the players who had been at FCA joined in, singing loudly and as well as a bunch of football players can sing. In an instant the room transformed from a quiet chapel to a raucous gathering of praise and worship. We stood up and locked arms, swaying with the verses and singing loud enough for people to hear us in the lobby. The Holy Spirit was moving through the room, and when we came around to the fourth verse, which is a repeat of the first, we sounded like we were part of the heavenly host. "I keep bringing souls to Jesus by the service that I yield!" I closed with a prayer, and we walked out of the room glowing like Moses coming down from the mountain.

On Saturday in the locker room before the game, Coach Tuberville reminded the team to play "with poise and confidence." He led the players onto the field, and at the moment when they usually ran out, somebody yelled, "Hey, let's hook up." Out in front the players locked arms, and instead of sprinting onto the field as usual, they walked with confidence—not the cocky stride of players who know how good they are, but quiet confidence knowing that God was ordering their steps. Several players told me later that they weren't even thinking about winning or losing at that point. They were just walking with God.

They might not have been thinking about winning, but by half-time they were beating Tennessee 31–3, and by the fourth quarter most of the Tennessee fans had left the stadium.

Every Friday night for the rest of the season, we sang "Hard Fighting Soldier" in the prayer room, and every Saturday we hooked up walking onto the field. The spirit of those moments spilled over everything we did on the practice field, in the film room, and on campus. Then in the locker room after the Ole Miss game, when we were 9–0 and champions of the Southeastern Conference Western Division, the players sang "War Eagle," then somebody yelled, "Hard Fighting Sol-dier." Instantly the locker room became the prayer room as players hooked up arm in arm and started singing and swaying and laughing in a thanksgiving spirit that poured out of us and filled that place. God had transformed us into witnesses, His message in the flesh for the world to see, because the following week on Coach Tuberville's televi-sion show, they showed that locker room scene.

> I keep on bringing souls to Jesus
> By the service that I give.

People sometimes talk about the 2004 team as if it were the first at Auburn to call upon the Lord. They should walk through the Lovelace Athletic Museum on campus and read the quotation that hangs from the ceiling:

> There are countless intangibles and unusual circumstances that lead to success or failure in almost every endeavor. I'm convinced that the underlying reason why Auburn attained the national championship in 1957 is a spiritual one.
> —Coach Ralph "Shug" Jordan

I never met Coach Jordan; he died the year before I came to Auburn as a student. But his statement reminds me that the Holy Spirit is eternal and has been on the Auburn University campus since its beginning in 1859, through good times and bad. What made 2004 special was the national attention an undefeated season brought to us, allowing us to glorify God before the nation.

29

A BIGGER STAGE

"You have been faithful with a few things; I will put you in charge of many things."

MATTHEW 25:21

Coach Tuberville had said in January 2004 that he believed God would transform the embarrassment of the Jetgate fiasco into an opportunity to "be given a stage where you can do more." As it turned out, the entire 13–0 season was filled with opportunities that culminated with Tommy being voted Coach of the Year by the American Football Coaches Association.

Ten days after beating Virginia Tech in the Sugar Bowl to complete the perfect season, Tommy stood on "a bigger stage" in front of more than five thousand coaches at the AFCA convention and told them his philosophy on coaching: "Everybody thinks your philosophy has to be about offense and defense. I've got news for you, when you become a head coach, offense and defense is a very small part of what you are going to do in the profession."

Tommy talked about off-season strength and conditioning, academics, and recruiting. He told the coaches about his beginnings as a high school football coach and the year he owned Tubby's Catfish Inn in Tennessee. "I learned about dealing with people in the restaurant business," he said.

But the real reason he was standing on that stage, he said, was because God had made it possible. "God gave me the opportunity to do what I have been doing the last few years, and I have tried to take full advantage of it," he said. Then he closed his speech by talking about our ministry:

> The last thing that I want to talk to you about is probably the most important thing that we've done at Auburn. . . . I am a big advocate of the FCA. Every player on your team needs somebody to talk to, somebody to relate to. Chette Williams works with our football team. He has made the biggest difference in my life, our coaches' lives, our families' lives, and our players' lives than anything I have ever seen.
>
> We're not talking about preaching to players and coaches. I'm talking about being a father figure. We have nineteen- to twenty-two-year-old young men that will come out, play hard, and run over each other. But when they have a problem, players will never come to you and tell you, "Coach, I have a problem."
>
> Chette talks to our players.
>
> We had a team this year at Auburn that was 13–0. You would think that the ego of that team would be phenomenal. Just the opposite. They loved each other. We had a football team that believed in each other, that loved each other every day in practice.

We had eighteen seniors who were the leaders of that bunch along with Chette Williams.

This is a tough generation that we are coaching, because two-thirds of the players we bring don't have a father. Many of them don't have mothers. We're actually their father and mother, and their counselors.

I would strongly urge you to look into the FCA, not just in spiritual needs but as a counselor for your players who come to practice every day to look for some guidance other than football. It will help you and the young men on your team grow. It's an amazing program.

Almost immediately after stepping down from the stage, Tommy had coaches asking him how they could create a program like ours for their players. He came home, and for days the phone rang as more coaches wanted to know what to do. Tommy quickly recognized the calls as a new opportunity: we could create a training program for chaplains who would serve other programs across the country. There was no way I could train chaplains and still meet the needs of our own guys, so he suggested Wes Yeary, his chaplain when he was coaching at Ole Miss.

"Coach Tuberville called and said the Lord had put this on his heart," Wes recalls, "and he said, 'You know, this thing is bigger than Ole Miss or Auburn. We have an opportunity to impact a lot of young men at other universities.' "

After praying and asking God for guidance, Wes accepted the challenge and became the nation's first FCA director of chaplaincy training at Auburn. He spent a year researching and planning, meeting with me and with chaplains at other schools, and in 2006 we had four interns on campus.

30

PRAISE REPORT AT TWENTY

Blessed are those who mourn, for they will be comforted.

MATTHEW 5:4

"I have a praise report," Alonzo Horton said. "My twentieth birthday was Wednesday."

Alonzo wasn't celebrating, and he wasn't expecting his teammates to break the quiet mood of the Friday night prayer room to sing "Happy Birthday." "I just praise God that my mom isn't mourning my twentieth birthday," he said, "because that's what she could have been doing this week."

Alonzo closed his eyes and listened in the silence to the click, click, click of the assault rifle that jammed. Then he spoke again. "It's not supposed to happen like that. You pull the trigger, and something's gonna come out."

It was Easter Sunday night in New Orleans. After attending church that morning with his mother, Alonzo had gone with two friends to Popeye's Chicken and walked from there to the Grand Theater to see a movie. On the way out he saw his thirteen-year-old sister, who lived with their father, walking quickly toward him. He hugged her and asked, "What's up?"

Some guys were trying to mess with her, she said, and she pointed to one man in a group of a dozen or so in their early twenties across the street. "No problem," Alonzo said, and he walked with his friends over to them.

The man who had been talking to Alonzo's sister straightened and tugged at his T-shirt as he approached. Alonzo didn't expect trouble right there on the street, but he didn't fear it. At six feet two, 215 pounds, he was rated the eleventh-best high school defensive end in the country and had signed with Auburn a month earlier. He could take care of himself on the field or in the street. "Hey, yo," he said to the man, "y'all don't be messing with my little sister. She's just thirteen—too young for you."

"Hey, no problem," the man said. "That's cool."

That was the end of it, and Alonzo and his friends walked back to his sister in front of the theater. He hadn't seen his sister in several weeks, and he enjoyed catching up with her. But twenty minutes later one of Alonzo's friends pointed down the street at the men, who were changing shirts. "They're gonna try to jump you," he told Alonzo. "They think you won't recognize them in different clothes."

"That's crazy," Alonzo said, but kept his eye on them. A minute later they were walking toward him. "You go on inside the movie," he told his sister, then he straightened up as the men crossed the street.

The one man stepped up and said, "Who the ---- are you to be talking to me?"

"Hey, I don't want any trouble," Alonzo said, still thinking he could talk his way out of a fight, but watching the man's right fist clinch. "I just told you you're too old for my sister."

The man swung at Alonzo, and Alonzo stepped toward him and hit him hard in the side of the head, knocking him toward the curb. The man didn't fall, and he came back at Alonzo, trying to tackle him with his shoulder. Alonzo forearmed him hard, then they both went down, Alonzo's elbow hitting the concrete hard.

A moment later somebody yelled, "Hey, cops!" and Alonzo saw everything falling apart. He'd be arrested and lose his scholarship and everything he had worked for. He pushed the guy away then jumped up and ran. The other man ran in the opposite direction, and a block down the street Alonzo was alone with his friends jogging toward Popeye's, thinking about his sister back at the theater.

An engine rumbled behind them, tires squealed, and Alonzo hopped onto the sidewalk as a car sped past then spun around. The door opened. Him again. Alonzo stood his ground as the driver stepped out. Then the man raised an assault rifle and aimed at Alonzo's face. *So this is how it ends*, Alonzo thought, and he inhaled slowly, his last breath coming more calmly than he had ever imagined.

"What's up now?" the man said, and he smiled a little and pulled the trigger. Nothing happened.

Alonzo exhaled. *Man, I'm alive!* he thought. *I'm alive!*

The man cursed and threw his gun into the car, and Alonzo and his friends sprinted past him toward Popeye's.

I knew those streets. I knew the Grand Theater where Alonzo had stood outside with his sister. New Orleans had been my city. For five years when he was growing up and I was in seminary and building a church in New Orleans, Alonzo and I lived less than two miles from each other. Maybe that's why he and I bonded quickly when he came to Auburn in June 2005. He came to our summer Bible study at the Buffalo Connection restaurant, and afterward he talked about home. He had grown up with a strong Christian mother and almost no contact with his father, who was in prison during what Alonzo called his "sponge years," ages six to eleven. "I could have gone bad," he said. "Some of my cousins on my father's side did. But my mother taught me right from wrong, and now I have to break the cycle for my little brothers."

Delorean and Jerry, who were six and seven years old—in their "sponge years"—lived with their father. Alonzo vowed to give them a good example to soak up—to help them find purpose and to understand the importance of an education. It would be hard from 350 miles away in Auburn.

Practice started in August, and throughout the month Alonzo worked hard on the scout team every day, focusing so much he didn't hear about the hurricane swirling in the Gulf of Mexico until Coach Terry Price pulled him aside and told him on Sunday afternoon, one day before Katrina slammed into New Orleans. After practice Alonzo came to my office, and we turned on the television. Hurricane Katrina was heading directly for the city, and the mayor had ordered an evacuation. We watched and prayed for Alonzo's family and friends to get out safely. On Monday the team didn't practice, but Alonzo came back to my office to watch the storm come ashore. Winds had eased up overnight, the reporters said, but thousands of people who had not fled the city were at risk.

We were still watching when Alonzo's cell phone rang. I could hear the woman's voice from across the room, almost hysterical. I watched Alonzo, sitting on the little sofa in my office, struggle to form the words that might comfort her.

"I'm with Brother Chette," he said, finally. "Let him pray with you."

Then he reached over to hand me the telephone. "It's my mother," he said, and in that moment I had nothing for her. So I just asked her questions and listened. Mrs. Horton told me she had fled her home to a hotel, and the wind was blowing so hard she thought it might blow away. The power was off, and outside the window was nothing but water. Her sister had refused to leave the house, but her niece had gone to a shelter at Abramson High School and hoped to find Jerry, Delorean, and their father there. As she spoke I began to pray silently that God would comfort her with His strength and His peace, and when she stopped talking, I prayed for those things aloud. Then I prayed for His protection over Mrs. Horton, her sister, and all of her family. I said *amen* and she said *amen*, and I think we both experienced peace in that moment together. I gave the phone back to Alonzo, and he told his mother that he loved her. Then he hit the *end* button, and she was gone. Alonzo's face was wet with tears. "Let's keep praying," I said, and I took his hand and prayed for God to strengthen Alonzo and, again, to protect his mother and family.

All day long teammates and coaches came in and out of my office as we watched television coverage. Alonzo left for a while to go to Coach Price's office, and when he came back, his phone rang again. He listened then gave the phone to me. His cousin was calling from the Abramson High gymnasium, and I could barely hear her over the crying and yelling in the background. All I could understand was, "We're not going to make it! We're not going to make it!" Only later would we learn that one of the levees had given way and water was rising fast. "God," I prayed over her screams, "protect these people, your children, from the storm. Give them strength, and help them find a way in the storm." Then the call dropped.

"She's with my brothers," Alonzo said. "She told me she saw them at the shelter. That's my high school. They're in our gym."

Sometime Monday night Alonzo and I said a final prayer, and he went home. Coach Tuberville had told him to take Tuesday off from practice, so I wasn't sure I would see him, but when I came up from the practice field, he was lying on the sofa in my office. He said he didn't want to miss practice again. The whole world was talking about his hometown. A sportswriter called him for an interview. Alonzo needed to get back onto the field so he could focus on anything other than his fears for a couple of hours a day.

Auburn's opening game was Saturday at home against Georgia Tech. Alonzo's first game. His first Tiger Walk. For a freshman football player it's one of the most exhilarating experiences of his life. Two hours before kickoff, thousands of people line Donahue Drive, and the players walk through a narrow corridor soaking in the cheers all the way from Sewell Hall to the stadium. If his family remained in the shelter surrounded by water, a cloud of fear would hang over the whole experience for Alonzo. "Saturday is Jerry's birthday," he said.

"What?" I asked.

"My little brother Jerry will be eight years old on Saturday."

Friday afternoon is the toughest day of the week for players who are not on the traveling squad. After working as hard as any man on the team, the guys who are injured and those being redshirted stay home while the rest of the team loads onto the bus. On Saturday home games they can make Tiger Walk and then dress out and stand on the sidelines, but NCAA rules say they can't go with the team to the hotel on Friday night. Alonzo was to be redshirted, so we left him behind.

Riding to the hotel I tried to think about my devotional, but all I could see was Alonzo. All through dinner I thought about him and wondered what he was doing at that moment. Only when Coach Tuberville signaled for me to give the two-minute warning so the players could finish dinner and settle down for the devotional did I begin to experience peace. I stood to speak and suddenly understood what Alonzo experienced when he stepped onto the practice field. The power of the Holy Spirit released me from my concerns for Alonzo and his family and allowed His Word to flow through me.

For our team Scripture in 2005 I had selected Philippians 3:13–14:

Forgetting what lies behind and reaching forward to what lies ahead, I press on toward the goal for the prize of the upward call of God in Christ Jesus. (NASB)

We had to put behind us the 2004 perfect season and focus on the task at hand. "We have to forget what happened last season," I said, "the same way we would forget a disastrous season. Just as our trials and tribulations can prevent us from reaching our future goals, so can our past successes if we dwell on them.

"Forgetting, reaching, pressing, that's what we have to be about this year."

When I finished, the players adjourned to their meetings, and an hour later we gathered in the prayer room. The first prayer lifted was for Alonzo's brothers, sister, and mother. Another player prayed for Alonzo—for strength, courage, and peace. After the *amen* we sat in the long, dark silence, and I wondered how dark that gymnasium in New Orleans must be and whether those scared little boys were sleeping or talking to people around them, whether they had food and water, how long they could last, when help would be coming.

Back in Auburn Alonzo had set the alarm on his telephone to ring at 12:01 a.m. to remind him of Jerry's birthday. At 11:58 p.m., the phone rang. He could hardly hear his cousin screaming over the commotion. "Somebody opened the door!" she cried. "They opened the door!" Water was rushing in, and she had lost Jerry and Delorean in the blackness. Now they were gone—swept away. That was all Alonzo heard before the call dropped. He put the phone down and hung his head.

> You have fed them with the bread of tears;
> You have made them drink tears by the bowlful.
> —Psalm 80:5

He waited until morning to call me, and I knew from his crying, before he could form the words, that they were gone. I held the phone and listened, waited, spoke his name softly, and prayed silently. When he was able, we prayed again, this time for God to receive Jerry and Delorean into His eternal loving embrace. "Brother Chette," Alonzo said finally, "I don't know what I have to live for. I was doing it all for them."

"You have to keep doing it for them," I said. "You have to honor them."

When we finished talking, I called Coach Tuberville. I knew he would want to call Alonzo and pray with him. I didn't know what Alonzo would do about the game, but when the players and coaches climbed down from the buses back in Auburn, Coach Tuberville saw him waiting off to the side. Tommy walked over and, without a word, hugged him. Players gathered around and cried with their brother, and then the band struck up "War Eagle," majorettes started their dance, Aubie and the cheerleaders waved to the crowd, and the team followed them down the hill through the cheering crowd to the stadium.

Alonzo wondered, *Is this what it's all about?*

Then something unexpected happened. From out of the crowd someone yelled, "We love you, Alonzo!" Another fan called him over and hugged him. Alonzo walked on and several more people called his name. They knew who he was—not just an Auburn Tiger, but Alonzo Horton, a hurting young man. His load lightened as he realized these people were helping him shoulder it. He told an ESPN reporter later, "Every step I took I started to feel better and better. I felt like I was walking to the light. Heaven was at that Tiger Walk and at that football field."

By Sunday Alonzo's mother and sister had evacuated to Atlanta, and Coach Tuberville gave him the day off to go visit. He came back on Tuesday, and when he wasn't on the practice field or in the weight room that week, he was visiting an evacuee relocation center that had been set up nearby. He encouraged the university to offer tours of campus and horse rides at the equestrian center for his displaced neighbors. In the midst of his grief, he was reaching out. But when I saw him alone, the smile didn't come so quickly.

Alonzo was overcoming his pain by serving others, but the wound would never heal completely. I reminded him that even Christ in His victory still bore the mark of the nails, and because He suffered, He understands. Likewise, Alonzo could reach the wounded with his unique understanding.

He came to my office every day and we prayed that there might be a mistake. After all, his brothers' bodies had not been found. But when he called a friend who was a New Orleans policeman, he learned that the evacuees at Abramson had drowned. A report on the Internet said three hundred bodies were still inside.

He tried to reach other friends and family to find out if they were safe, but reaching them, even on cell phones, was difficult because of the massive infrastructure damage in Louisiana. A week later on Sunday afternoon after practice, he was in Wal-Mart with a couple of teammates when he reached a cousin and was telling him about Jerry and Delorean.

"No," his cousin said. "They got out!"

"No way!" Alonzo cried.

"Yeah, hold on."

Standing in the aisle at Wal-Mart, Alonzo began to shake as he waited on hold for his cousin to make the call. A moment later he heard his father's voice and then both of his little brothers'. "Where are you?" Alonzo asked.

"Houston," his father said. "We got out."

"How? When?"

But the call dropped before they could answer. Alonzo didn't care. *They're alive!*

Alonzo stood before his teammates two days after his twentieth birthday, a year after Hurricane Katrina. His home and his high school are gone. His old neighborhood lies in ruins. His mother's sister drowned in the storm. Yet he praises God for strength in his trials, and he embraces the promise of Deuteronomy 20:1:

> When you go to war against your enemies and see horses and chariots and an army greater than yours, do not be afraid of them, because the LORD your God, who brought you up out of Egypt, will be with you.

31

AN AUDIENCE OF ONE

Whatever you do, work at it with all your heart, as working for the Lord, not for men, since you know that you will receive an inheritance from the Lord as a reward. It is the Lord Christ you are serving.

COLOSSIANS 3:23–24

"You ready?" Coach Tuberville asked.

"Ready," I said.

He stood and raised his hand, and the hotel banquet room quickly fell silent. A moment earlier the entire team, coaches, and support staff had been clanking plates and glasses, talking loudly and laughing. Tommy got their attention and sat down, and I stood. "Two-minute warning," I said. "Go get your ice cream, then come back and turn your chairs around."

"That's right," Jonathan Palmer yelled, "turn your tables around," and the whole room started laughing. It was an old joke—a year earlier I had misspoken and told the team to turn their tables instead of their chairs, and ever since then Tim Duckworth and J.P., the big right side of our offensive line, had raced each other to see who could say it first.

It was Friday night, just a few hours away from Saturday's opening game against Washington State University, and we had left town. This was part of a home-game tradition that began when the NCAA told universities they could no longer maintain a single dormitory for scholarship athletes. On Friday afternoon the team loaded on buses and rode to an out-of-town hotel for the night, bringing everybody together and helping them focus on the task at hand.

The official schedule called for dinner followed by offensive and defensive team meetings and curfew; then on Saturday morning, a pregame meal and the trip back to campus for the Tiger Walk into Jordan-Hare Stadium. The players had prepared themselves physically in the days and weeks leading up to this moment, and tonight they would make final mental preparations. Coach Tuberville believed they would not be ready to play on Saturday, however, until their hearts were prepared as well. He set aside a half hour after dinner for me to bring them an inspirational message and an hour after team meetings to gather for a voluntary time of prayer together. This is a reflection of Coach Tuberville's commitment to building the spiritual lives of young men. He puts God's message right up front with devotionals and prayers scheduled at times when they will have the maximum impact.

All of the coaches, graduate assistants, staff members—even the bus driver and state patrol escorts—were in the room finishing dinner. Tonight, for the eighth straight year and with God's leading, I would be giving the Scripture for the year, words we would carry with us for the next four months and, perhaps, for the rest of our lives.

On this Friday night at the beginning of the 2006 season, I believed God was telling us, "Do everything you do for Me—not for the 87,000 people in the stands, not for the media or the pro scouts, not for your family or your girlfriend, but for Me." God wanted us to conduct ourselves on the field as if Jordan-Hare Stadium were completely empty but for Him watching from His fifty-yard-line seat. An Audience of One.

"For guys who love the Lord," I said, "that means making a total commitment—selling out for God. Whatever you do on the field, you do it unto Him, giving him 110 percent, because He's watching."

Over the course of the season we would play thirteen games, winning eleven and losing two. On the field and in our lives we sometimes forgot who we were playing for. We neglected our Audience. Along the way, however, the Holy Spirit stepped into our lives and gave us more victories than I count. Here is a small sample—thirteen wins we experienced.

— ONE —

Twenty players gathered around a pile of hot wings for our first Bible study of the summer, and I started telling them about Abram and his brother Lot. God had blessed them both so much, their herds had grown to the point that they had to separate so they would have enough grazing land. Abram took the plain of Jordan, while Lot took his herds toward Sodom. "We move closer and closer to sin," I said, using Lot's relocation choice as an illustration, "and before we realize it, sin takes us over."

At that point Travaris Robinson spoke up. T-Rob was an All-Conference safety at Auburn in 2002 and played in the NFL with Tampa Bay and Atlanta before a knee injury ended his career. He came back to Auburn to complete his degree and work with the coaches as a volunteer student assistant. "Everybody is so eager to get to the NFL and get that money," he said, "but even if you make it today, you don't know if you'll be on the team tomorrow. Look at me.

"The NFL is a business. Auburn is a family. People care about you like a brother. But even here there is so much temptation. You come here to play football, and people treat you special. They put you on a pedestal, and pretty soon you think you're invincible. You're skipping class, creating bad relationships, and bringing negative energy to the team or the community."

On the spur of the moment, T-Rob was preaching a sermon, and the guys were totally focused on him. They had so much respect for a man who had made it to the League, and in that moment I knew God had sent another messenger to speak to us.

— TWO —

Steve Gandy and I prayed together on the sidelines of Jordan-Hare Stadium before the opening game while the team went through pre-game drills. Back during two-a-days, Gandy had taken a hit to the thigh and had gone down with a deep bruise. He iced it down, but later that night it started swelling. It got so big he thought his leg would literally burst. He called one of the trainers, who called the team physician, who told Gandy to get to the emergency room immediately.

The hit had caused acute compartment syndrome, which is swelling so great that it can collapse the blood vessels, leading to loss of the leg or even death. Emergency surgery—an incision from his hip to his knee—allowed the fluid to drain, but doctors told Gandy he wouldn't be playing football this season. He refused to give in, though, and he worked hard with strength coach Kevin Yoxall.

In our Friday night prayer meeting, we had prayed for Gandy, who had become an inspiration to the guys on the field with his hard work and his own prayers. Now as I sat on the bench before the game with this young man, the Lord led me to ask him to offer the pregame prayer in the locker room. His gratitude and commitment to the Lord, even as he was in his street clothes surrounded by teammates preparing to play, touched me, and I know they affected the players.

Three weeks later during our prayers on Friday night, Gandy was able to praise God for His healing touch. The next day he proved the doctors wrong by suiting up and starting against Buffalo, finishing the game with five tackles.

— THREE —

All of the coaches have FCA Bibles with a year's worth of devotionals. They keep them on their desks for their quiet time. (And there isn't much of it during the season.) Each week before their staff meeting, Tommy invites me to lead a brief devotional, and I usually select that day's reading from the FCA Bible as a starting point. I wonder sometimes as I stand in front of them what the coaches are thinking. They're under so much pressure to prepare for the next game, and there is so little time, they must be working out game plans and moving players around in their heads.

Early one morning I passed offensive coordinator Al Borges in the hallway, and he looked excited about something. "Did you read today's devotional?" he asked. "Is that the one you're using? Or yesterday's. It was good too."

Wow! I thought. Coach Borges had stepped out of his game preparation and into God's Word. I felt the smile spread across my face. We all need an encourager, and Coach Borges became mine that morning.

— FOUR —

Karibi Dede and Brant Haynie, teammates for four years, sat in my office reflecting on their time at Auburn. You probably don't know much about Haynie. He was a walk-on safety who didn't even get his name on a locker until midway through his sophomore year. Dede, on the other hand, was a four-year starter and one of Auburn's most recognized defensive players. Who looks up to whom?

"People look at players who get their names in the paper, the stars," Dede said, "and think that's who the other players look to for guidance or aspire to. Not me. I look to godly people like Haynie and [deep snapper] Pete Compton."

"I had no idea," Haynie said.

Some kids walk on at Auburn hoping to prove to the coaches that they're the next Bo Jackson. Not Haynie. "I was not naive about my role on the team," he said. "I knew there was a reason Auburn didn't offer me a scholarship. I don't have the athletic ability of some of these other guys. But I knew if I came in here and worked hard, I had enough gifts to contribute in some way."

He never read about his contribution in the newspaper. As a senior he remained third on the depth chart at safety. But in the final weeks of his football career, Haynie was blessed to see how God had used him to contribute to the spiritual lives of his teammates.

— FIVE —

On the Friday night before the LSU game, Dr. Danny Wood, pastor of Shades Mountain Baptist Church in Birmingham, gave the team devotional and took us back nearly three thousand years to show us what it really means to be a hero. He spoke about three of King David's mighty men, who risked their lives to break through enemy lines and bring their leader a drink of water from the well of Bethlehem, his hometown.

Then Dr. Wood told the story with a different perspective: "Suppose Auburn had been laid siege and you were hiding out in Opelika, and Coach Tuberville said, 'If I could have just one thing in the world, it would be a cold glass of lemonade from Toomer's Corner.'"

As he spoke he brought out a cold glass of lemonade from behind the lectern. Holding the lemonade up, he continued, "Which of you, out of your love and loyalty for him, would walk through the night back to Auburn, fight through the enemy lines to get downtown, wake up the owner of Toomer's Drugstore to make a glass of fresh lemonade, and then hustle that lemonade back to Coach Tub?"

I wonder sometimes about the impact of our words during our devotional time—whether the guys remember or take them to heart. Well, on Saturday morning in the locker room as the players were getting ready to go out for stretches, I overheard Tim Duckworth tell another player, "I want to be one of the three." Dr. Wood had inspired a hero.

— SIX —

As soon as all the players and coaches come back to the locker room after every game, Coach Tuberville offers a quick word, then he asks me to pray before he talks with the players at greater length.

After the LSU game, which Auburn won 10–7 by stopping LSU at the four-yard line as time ran out, the stadium was still rocking above us as Tommy let the guys celebrate a great victory. When everybody finally settled down, I expected him to tell them, "Great game," or offer some other compliment before asking me to pray. Instead he said, "Today we played for an Audience of One. Chette . . ."

I felt a sudden lightness. In the midst of a huge win, the head coach was thinking about—and talking to the team about—our Lord. What a cause for celebration!

The next week Tommy reflected on that moment and his statement. "That's what we want these players to understand. We're not playing for each other. We're not playing for our families. After a game like that, the first One to get recognition should be God. He allowed us to play that game. He allowed us to play to the best of our abilities. He allowed us to play within ourselves. And we'd better give the praise to God."

— SEVEN —

During a Friday night prayer meeting Coach Eddie Gran told the team about his friend Travis Rabren, a young man whose daughters are playmates with Eddie and Rosemary's daughters. Travis was diagnosed with liver cancer and was undergoing chemotherapy. Every Friday for eleven straight weeks, the chemicals had made Travis so sick he couldn't get out of bed until Sunday. The ordeal was draining his energy and his optimism.

Will Herring asked another player to pray for Travis, and we bowed and held hands and asked God to comfort and strengthen him, to walk alongside his wife and daughters, and to guide the doctors in their treatment.

The next afternoon after the game, Eddie was leaving the stadium, and he was surprised to see Travis sitting in a chair surrounded by his family. "Hey, buddy," Eddie said. "How you doing?"

"Great," Travis answered. "They tried a new kind of chemo on me yesterday, and I woke up this morning with a new energy."

Eddie had to stop and swallow hard before he could speak. Finally he was able to say, "Do you know you had fifty kids praying for you last night?" Then neither man could speak.

Back in the prayer room the next Friday night with tears in his eyes, Eddie offered his praise and Travis's thanks to the team. "It was a pretty intense moment," he told us. "The chemotherapy had really been tearing him up, and on Saturday he was able to go to the game and stay the whole time. Then on Sunday morning he went to church with his family, and that afternoon he went dove hunting."

"Praise report on three. Praise report on three," Karibi Dede announced. *Clap. Clap. Clap.* "Amen."

— EIGHT —

Fred Stokes's sons know all about the National Football League. Their father played defensive end for ten years in the League. In Super Bowl XXVI with the Washington Redskins, Fred had six tackles, a quarterback sack, and a fumble recovery.

"But I'm just their dad," Fred said at our team dinner on Friday night before the Buffalo game. "They want to meet the *real* stars."

"Where's Courtney Taylor?" one of the boys asked, as if on cue.

"Standing right behind you," Fred said.

The boy turned and stared. It really was *the* Courtney Taylor.

I had asked Fred, a committed Christian, to offer our after-dinner devotional, and I invited him to bring his boys, ages nine and twelve, with him. The boys were starstruck as they stood among players they had seen only on television. Then they came with us into the prayer room and watched these same players humbling themselves before God, giving Him the glory for their gifts. If only more young men could join us in the prayer room . . .

— NINE —

That same night Fred told the team about his line coach at Georgia Southern University, Hugh Nall, now the offensive line coach at Auburn. Coach Nall had been the meanest, cussingest, toughest coach Fred had ever known. More than once Fred had considered telling Coach Nall where to stick his football and walking off the field forever. Then Fred got into some trouble, big trouble with the university, and it was Coach Nall who stood at his side and convinced the school to give him another chance.

Fred had no idea that his nemesis cared so much about him. That moment changed the way he saw his coach and inspired him to refocus his life. Fred also had no idea of the impact of his words to us on that Friday night. Coach Nall was on a recruiting trip watching high school football, so he couldn't hear what his former player had to say. But one young man in the room listened closely. Two days earlier the player had argued with Coach Nall and left the field so angry that he thought about leaving Auburn. Listening to Fred, he wondered if there might really be another side to Coach Nall. The next morning he found Coach Nall before the game, and they talked and were reconciled.

How many times does the Lord use us in ways we don't even realize?

— TEN —

The Georgia game (a 37–15 loss) was such a miserable experience for players, coaches, and fans that it would have been easy to lose focus.

Quentin Groves went down with an injury in the second half, and the players might have hung their heads and said, "It's over." But Tristan Davis didn't miss a beat. He immediately ran down the sidelines in front of the bench yelling, "Come on! Come on! We've got to pray for Q!" Within seconds he had forty guys on their knees praying for their brother on the field.

The injury was minor, and Quentin was able to go back into the game later. But the point was, the players remembered, even in the midst of defeat. "We know there is power through prayer," Tristan said later. "That's always a big part of our team, no matter what."

— ELEVEN —

The Tennessee Titans had signed Wayne Dickens as an undrafted free agent in May 2006, but Wayne felt the Lord calling him into ministry. He left Tennessee and came back to Auburn, where he had played defensive tackle, and joined the FCA staff working with high schools in east Alabama. Wayne has direct contact with young athletes across the region, praying and praising God with them. God is also ministering to Wayne through the athletes. He came back to the office one afternoon after visiting a high school huddle and said they had modeled their game-day routine based on Auburn.

"They were hooking up coming out onto the field and praying for each other during the game," he said. "It made me feel good to know that what we were doing wasn't just for ourselves—that God was using it to build up others who were watching us."

— TWELVE —

Throughout the season Wes Yeary, Director of FCA Chaplain Training and Development, worked closely with four interns training to serve as FCA chaplains in 2007. Coach Tuberville was right when he told Wes, "This thing is bigger than Auburn or Ole Miss." God is using Wes to take His Word to athletes we will never know in this world. Interns James and Jasmine Cochran are serving the Lord at Southern Mississippi University, Taylor Stewart is at Georgia Tech, and Carly Thomas has stayed at Auburn to work with athletes through our FCA program. They are better prepared to meet challenges that Wes and I never knew we would face, all because the Lord created a bigger stage through the commitment of Coach Tuberville.

— THIRTEEN —

In eight seasons since coming back to Auburn, I had retraced almost every step from my years as a student. The one place I had not returned to, however, was the little pond at the bottom of the waterfall at Chewacla State Park, six miles out from town.

I had accepted Christ as my Savior and had joined a Bible study group that my teammate Todd Burkhalter was leading. Toward the end of the year we were reading about baptism, and I wanted to be baptized to mark my profession of faith. Kyle Collins and the other guys in the group agreed; we would all be baptized.

We drove out to Chewacla, and the day was as beautiful as Easter morning, with a bright blue sky and that water sparkling over the rocks into the pool. We stepped out into the creek like we were stepping into the Jordan River, and I could hear the words of the apostle Peter: "Repent and be baptized, every one of you, in the name of Jesus Christ for the forgiveness of your sins. And you will receive the gift of the Holy Spirit" (Acts 2:38).

In 2006 I told Wayne Dickens and Alonzo Horton the story, and they wanted to go see the place. They too were ready to be baptized. We rode out to Chewacla and climbed down over the rocks and followed the little trail to the spot. They immediately said that's where they wanted to be baptized, and we began to make our plans. But it was November, and they wanted their families to witness their baptism, so an outdoor event didn't seem practical. Instead we went to the White Street Baptist Church, where I have baptized so many other players, and the event was just as beautiful, just as meaningful. Dr. Johnny Green, the pastor at White Street, is also Auburn's dean of students and chaplain of the men's basketball team. Johnny has provided a church home for dozens of players and thousands of students through the years.

I don't baptize as many players as I did in the early days of our ministry because so many of them now come to Auburn already having committed their lives to the Lord. Today I spend more time mentoring and shepherding. Yet my greatest joy will always be hearing young men like Wayne and Alonzo profess their belief in Christ as they step down into the water.

32

SENDING FORTH

Be on the alert, stand firm in the faith, act like men, be strong. Let all that you do be done in love.

1 Corinthians 16:13–14 (NASB)

I stood in front of the team at the Cotton Bowl, the final college game for twenty-two seniors. Like a parent who watches a child leave home, I wondered if we had done all we could for these men in the short time they had been with us. What else could I say in just a few minutes to prepare them for what would lie ahead? Choosing to keep the message simple, I turned to 1 Corinthians 16:13-14 for a reminder to the players—and to me.

Be on the alert

I lined up on the kickoff return team at the thirty-five-yard line three yards outside the left hash mark. It was 1983, my junior year at Auburn. The crowd at Jordan-Hare Stadium was on its feet yelling "WAAAR EAGLE" as the kicker sent the ball sailing high toward

Lionel James, waiting at the goal line. I sprinted back to the fifteen and turned around, lining up shoulder-to-shoulder with two teammates to form a blocking wedge. Lionel yelled, "GO!" and we ran full speed up field. Twenty yards ahead of us the front line took out their men, and more opponents ran toward us. Two men slammed in to the right side of the wedge, but I was still on my feet. Lionel would be coming my way, trying to make it to the sideline. Their big defensive end drew a bead on our 150-pound Number 6, knowing he would need every bit of concentration to tackle Lionel in the open field. At the last moment the tackler saw me coming, but it was too late. I slammed into him hard and laid him out flat just as Lionel ran past us.

That's the way Satan works. We think we have our eye on the target, and from somewhere out of the blue, *wham*, he knocks us flat on our back.

Be alert. Put your head on a swivel. Satan is no little red imp standing on your shoulder. He's strong and beautiful, smart and appealing, and most of all, he's cunning. He'll attack every important relationship in your life, especially your marriage. Don't get blindsided.

Stand firm in the faith

You never stood firm by yourself on the football field. If you had tried, the other team would have run you over. You were able to stand firm because you were hooked up with your brothers. Your strength was in your combined power. That's how you won thirty-three games over the last three years.

Now you're going into the world, and Peter reminds you that you are not the only one facing trials: "Your brothers throughout the world are undergoing the same kind of sufferings" (1 Peter 5:9). But they are no longer beside you facing the enemy together. You're scattered. You're going to have to stand alone.

Stand firm even if it means standing alone. Don't be afraid to be different. Remember, though, that you will never be totally alone if you hook up with the Holy Spirit. That's where your strength will come from.

> It is God who arms me with strength
> and makes my way perfect.
> He makes my feet like the feet of a deer;
> he enables me to stand on the heights.
> He trains my hands for battle;
> my arms can bend a bow of bronze.
> You give me your shield of victory,
> and your right hand sustains me;
> you stoop down to make me great.
> —Psalm 18:32-35

Act like men, be strong

The Greek word is actually *adults*, but the point is clear. Grow up! You're finishing college now. Put away childish things. Stop making excuses.

There's a dramatic moment in the movie "Black Hawk Down" where U.S. soldiers are pinned down by gunfire in the streets of Mogadishu. Ranger Lt. Col. Danny McKnight leads a Humvee unit in for a rescue, taking casualties all over. McKnight pulls a dead soldier from behind the steering wheel of a Humvee and orders another soldier, "Get in the truck and drive."

The soldier replies, "But I'm shot, colonel."

"We're all shot!" McKnight says. "Get in the truck and drive!"

People will remember the 2006 season for all the injuries to key players. I wish everybody could have seen the brace and tape Brandon Cox wore on his leg for most of the 2006 season. Do you think his pain went away when he stepped onto the field? No way! He played through his pain by drawing strength and love from his teammates. Brandon and Kenny Irons, with his injured foot, got the most media attention, but many others played through serious pain.

When you're wounded out the real world, when you've messed up so bad you think you can never recover or be forgiven, nobody's going to be cheering for you. Still, you have to get back in the game. No excuses. Get back in there!

Let all that you do be done in love

Love is the reason I am who I am. I was the troublemaker. The bad attitude. The lost cause. Then I became an instant convert when Coach Dye kicked me off the team. *How convenient!* people must have thought. When I told Kyle Collins I had changed, he had little reason to believe I really had. He and Todd Burkhalter could have waited for me to prove myself through my actions. After all, I had been so disrespectful of both of them, I might as well have spit in their face. Why should they suddenly let me be their friend? Yet they did, without patronizing me while looking for the evidence of my conversion. They even invited me to their parents' homes on weekends.

There's a beautiful scene near the beginning of *Les Miserables* when Jean Valjean, just released from prison, steals silverware from a kind bishop who had taken him in for the night. The police capture Valjean and bring him to the bishop, who insists Valjean is no thief. The silverware was a gift, the bishop says, and he meant for Valjean to have two silver candlesticks as well. The bishop dismisses the police, leaving Valjean standing at the door holding the silver, trembling and confused. Then the bishop steps closer to Valjean and says, "Do not forget, never forget, that you have promised to use this money in becoming an honest man." Jean Valjean didn't remember making such a promise, but he said nothing. The bishop continued, "Jean Valjean, my brother, you no longer belong to evil, but to good. It is your soul that I buy from you; I withdraw it from black thoughts and the spirit of perdition, and I give it to God."

That was the Christlike love my new brothers exhibited toward me. They didn't ask me to prove myself worthy. They just loved me.

Christ's love changed me. My friends' love upheld me. Then they challenged me to "Go and do likewise" (Luke 10:37), and it has made all the difference.